PSYCHOLOGICAL ATLAS

PSYCHOLOGICAL ATLAS

BY

DAVID KATZ

UNIVERSITY OF STOCKHOLM

WITH 400 ILLUSTRATIONS

PHILOSOPHICAL LIBRARY

NEW YORK

TABLE OF CONTENTS

FOREWORD

Pictures and diagrams reach across the barriers of language and differing modes of thought, and thereby people are brought into a community of understanding. For many years it has been the good fortune of Professor David Katz, of the University of Stockholm, to be invited to speak to diverse groups of people about the methods and the subject matter of the science of psychology. Thus he discovered that, no matter how the members of his audience differed in comprehension of his language, the use of graphic materials aroused their interest and served to illustrate his points. Over a period of many years he has collected many graphic materials whereby to illuminate these popular lectures as well as to stimulate his university students to acquire a deep store of knowledge about principles and methods in the study of behavior.

The translator has wisely kept some of the "Old World flavor" in many of the concise explanatory notes. To the professional American psychologist many of the pictures and diagrams will appear quaintly amusing. He will be interested to learn what foreign students of psychology learn about the work of American psychologists. A number of the pictures are the common property of all psychologists, but most of them are rarely found in American books. Students of psychology are certain to discover that this atlas furnishes material for many a pleasant and stimulating hour.

Philip Lawrence Harriman,
Bucknell University

INTRODUCTION

In many fields of science the atlas has proved to be a useful device for interesting the young student. Courses like geography, zoology, botany, anatomy, and history of art necessitate the use of graphic materials. No one has hitherto brought together within the covers of a single volume the interesting and useful pictures which relate to various phases of psychology. Consequently, this atlas, which represents the first attempt to organize a collection of graphic material, should meet a genuine need.

The book is intended to stimulate an interest in psychology. In other words, the primary intent of the author is not that of making a contribution to science, but that of arousing a zeal for the study of psychology. For many years he has taken advantage of every opportunity to illustrate, by demonstrations and pictures, his lectures and discussions in the classroom. As a result, he has accumulated a large number of pictures. Even when lecturing before gatherings not well-versed in the author's language, he has found that the intelligibility of pictures and diagrams transcended linguistic barriers.

Now these materials are presented to American students of psychology. The general reader may find this atlas as interesting as the classroom student. The pictures certainly demonstrate how broad is the scope of psychology; hence they may serve to counteract the influence of evanescent interests in such fields as abnormal psychology or child development. Here, in short, is an eloquent demonstration of the breadth of the field of psychology.

Not all branches of psychology can be adequately illustrated by pictures and diagrams. To represent in graphic form some of the more abstruse topics would require the use of cumbersome diagrams and pedantic explanations. If that were done, the atlas would defeat its purpose and become a sterile textbook. Likewise, it has been necessary to disregard the matter of coherence. Groupings of pictures are, necessarily, arbitrary procedures; and the user of this atlas may wish to re-organize the arrangements.

The pictures are numbered sequentially, and the explanatory comments — necessarily brief and inadequate — are given in Part I. By intent, these notes have been made brief. They are intended merely to stimulate the young student to relate this textbook knowledge to a concrete situation. These pictures have been chosen from many sources. Some are the common property of all psychologists; hence no credit is given. Many of the pictures have been drawn from rare books. Some pictures, unfortunately, the author has been unable to trace.

David Katz
University of Stockholm

PART ONE

I. GENERAL PSYCHOLOGY

Physiological Foundations

1*. Lateral view of the left hemisphere of the brain. The following motor centers are indicated: eye movement (*Augendrehung*), movement of head (*Kopfdrehung*), Broca's speech area (*Sprache*), writing (*Schreiben*), facial muscles (*Mundfazialis*), tongue (*Zunge*), larynx (*Kehlkopf*), mastication (*Kauen*), esophagus (*Schlund*), leg (*Bein*), and arm (*Arm*). The following centers for sensory functions are indicated: area for general sensation (*Körperfühlsphäre*), visuo-sensory areas (*optisches Sprachzentrum; optische Erinnerungsbilder*), and audio-sensory area (*akustisches Sprachzentrum*).

2. The medial surface of the right hemisphere. The following centers are indicated: area for general sensation (*Körperfühlsphäre*), olfaction (*Riechen*), gustation (*Schmecken*), and vision (*Sehen*).

3. The autonomic nervous system and its relation to the central nervous system, the duct and the ductless glands, and the visceral organs.

4. A section of the spinal chord; *cp,* afferent (sensory) nerve; *g,* ganglion; *s,* synapse; *cf,* efferent (motor) cell.

5. Schematic representation of the electroencephalogram, which records brain waves.

---

* The numbering of the descriptions in Part One corresponds to the numbers of the pictures and the diagrams in Part Two.

6. Two different types of brain waves; *A*, the Alpha rhythm; *Z*, the time line; and *B*, the Beta wave.

Olfaction, Gustation, and Hunger

7. Schematic representation of the olfactory cells and the supporting tissues.

8. Henning's olfactory sensation prism, the six basic odors being as follows: resinous, burnt, putrid, spicy, flowery, fruity.

9. Papilla and taste bud of the human tongue.

10. Diagram of the upper surface of the tongue, showing the regions not yielding the four basic tastes. The dots in circles at the top represent the circumvallate papillae; . . . . encloses the area insensitive to bitter; ———— encloses the area insensitive to sweet; ' ' ' ' the area insensitive to salty; and ooooo the area insensitive to sour. The zone filled with dots is totally insensitive to taste.

11. The taste tetrahedron. There are four basic taste sensations: sweet, sour, bitter, and salty.

12.–13. Cannon, an American physiologist, devised a method for studying the contractions of the stomach in hunger. He had a subject swallow a rubber ball connected to a drum (*M*). Thus, the rhythmic contractions were recorded on a kymograph (*K*). The inhalation-expiration ratio was measured by a pneumograph (*P*). The subject indicated his awareness of hunger pangs by pressing a telegraph key. A section of the kymographic record is shown in diagram 13.

14.–15. Succi, an Italian professional faster, before and after twenty-nine days of abstinence from food.

16. Even at the same intensities of hunger, a hen will eat more from a large heap of food than from a small one. These tests were performed daily; small and large piles of food being used alternately, the hunger intensity of the hen being kept constant.

4

Cutaneous sensations

17. The spots indicate minute areas on the backs of the fourth and fifth fingers which are sensitive to cold. Not all points on the surface of the skin are equally sensitive to stimuli of heat, cold, pressure, or pain.

18. Sensitivity of body surface to heat. The darker the area, the greater the sensitivity.

19. Areas of the body at which vibrations are sensed while singing. The drawing shows the degrees of the damping of the vibrations (expressed in *nepers*) in various bodily regions.

20. Vibrators are used in a study of the vibratory sensations. These devices relay graded vibrations to the body. When the subject holds a vibrator in each hand, he can recognize the difference if one hand receives the vibrations 1/10,000th of a second before the other.

21. The bar-triangle experiment. Three wooden bars are arranged to form an isosceles triangle open at the vertex. The subject places his hands on the base of the triangle, and the experimenter gently taps one of the bars near the open vertex. The subject can recognize, by vibration sense, whether the shaking reaches him from the right or the left. This apparatus has been used in studies of the "vibration sense."

Audition and the sense of equilibrium

22. A cross-section of the human ear. 1, auditory nerve; 2, inner auditory canal; 3, utricle; 4, one of the semicircular canals; 5, saccule; 6, cochlea; 7, ductus endolymphaticus; 8, saccus endolymphaticus; 9, perilymph space; 10, osseous labyrinth; 11, petrous bone; 12, oval window; 13, round window; 14, auricle; 15 and 16, cartilaginous and osseous parts of the external auditory canal; 17, tympanic membrane; 18, malleus; 19, incus; 20, stirrup; 21, 22, and 23, middle ear.

23. Diagrammatic representation of tones. Musical tones differ in intensities, timbre, and pitches. *O* represents the upper limit of hearing — about 40,000 vibra-

tions a second; U, the lower limit — about 20 vibrations a second. High tones (H) are light in volume; low tones (T) are heavy and massive. The approximate position of the tonal qualities of certain vowels and consonants is indicated.

24. Analysis of a musical sound, consisting of tone and overtone.

25. The inner ear includes the sense organs for balance: the vestibular apparatus and the semicircular canals. These receptors may be stimulated by rotating the subject in a revolving chair.

Vision and optical illusions

26. Cross section of the human eye: s, sclera; b, cornea; f, conjunctiva; a, crystalline lens; k, nodal points; c, posterior chamber; g, choroid tunic; h, ciliary muscle; b, iris; i, retina; p, yellow spot (macula lutea); and, d, optic nerve.

27. Examples of stages in the evolution of the human eye. A, nautilus; B, phyllodoce; C, nauphanta; and, D, cuttlefish.

28. To locate the blind-spot, close the right eye, hold the book about a foot away, fixate the left eye on the upper cross. Observe that the large circle disappears, though the smaller circles remain in the field of vision. Now shift the fixation point to the lower cross and observe that the large circle reappears. This phenomenon is caused by the blind-spot (Mariotte's circle), which is the point at which the optic nerve emerges into the eyeball. The spot is about 1/17th of an inch in diameter.

29. The perimeter, an instrument used in determining the color zones of the retina.

30. The results of an eye-test by the perimeter are recorded on a chart: F, fixation point; B, location of blind-spot; the line, the boundaries of the field of vision.

31. The color pyramid, a tridimensional, schematic representation of basic colors: V, white; S, black; $rö$, red; bl, blue; gr, green; and gu, yellow.

32. A simple device for illustrating positive after-images. On one side of a card letters are printed right-side-up, and on the other upside down; the card is rotated by strings, and an image of the word persists. This phenomenon is also called the terminal lag of a visual sensation.

33. The histology of the retina: St (*Stäbchen*), rods; Z (*Zapfen*), cones; G 1, G 2 neurons.

34. Simultaneous brightness-contrast. The small circles are of equal brightness, and so are the angles (d); but the contrasting backgrounds make them appear unequal in brightness.

35. Each ring is of the same degree of brightness throughout, but the contrasts make the inner half of each ring look brighter and the outer half darker. This is called marginal contrast.

36. If the eyes are fixated at the center, gray areas appear where the white lines bisect. This illusion is attributable to the contrast effect, which is especially strong in the lateral plane of the retina.

37. Helmholtz's chessboard design. In order to make the lines of a chessboard appear straight, they must be curved like those in the figure. If this design were enlarged sevenfold, the lines would appear straight when viewed with one eye from a distance of eight inches.

38.–39. *Astigmatism* literally means that a point (*stigma*) is not correctly perceived. Defective curvature in one or more of the refractory portions of the eye is the cause. It has been suggested that certain irregularities in the figures painted by El Greco are due to the artist's astigmatism, but the hypothesis has not been proved.

40. The Müller-Lyer illusion. Actually, the horizontal lines are of equal length.

41. Zöllner illusion. The vertical lines are parallel, but the short bisecting lines make them appear to slant.

42. Hering illusion. This, also, indicates that acute angles are over-estimated, and obtuse angles are underestimated. The lines in the upper and the lower representations are parallel.

43. The horizontal line running through the middle of the drawing appears to rise towards the left. The explanation is that each pair of contiguous squares is perceived as a unit; and, as a result of the emphasis thus placed upon their diagonal, they appear to be twisted clockwise. The illusion is caused by the cumulative effect of this torsion motive.

44. Lipps illusion. The central oblique lines are parallel, though they do appear to diverge. The illusion is attributable to the repetition of contrast effects.

45. The slant of the individual strokes which compose the letters is transferred to the letters. If the figure is viewed from a distance, the illusion vanishes.

46. You believe that you are looking at spirals, but actually they are circles. The brighter outlines of the circles make them appear to bend outwards, and the darker outlines, inwards. The cumulative effect of these alternate lines makes the illusion so obvious.

47. Curvature contrast. The inner lines are identical.

48. The distance from 1 to 2, from 3 to 4, and from 4 to 5 is the same; but that between 1 and 2 appears to be the shortest. The explanation lies in the fact that we do not attend to the diameters of the lower circles in estimating the distance.

49. Sander's illusion. The diagonals of the two joined parallelograms on the right are of identical length, but the diagonal of the larger parallelogram seems to be longer. The judgment depends upon the relative size of the figure. Compare the length of the lines in the parallograms with those in the triangle at the left.

50. The man in the distance appears to be larger than the boy, though both are of the same height. The illusion is due to the perspective effect.

51. If you rotate this picture rapidly, the striped disks will appear to move in the same direction and the cogwheel in the opposite direction. When it is stopped, we get the impression that it is revolving in the opposite direction. This illusion is mainly the result of contrast effects.

52. Apparatus for the demonstration of apparent movement. The disk on the rotator is slowly revolved for about a minute. When it is stopped, we get the

impression that it is revolving in the opposite direction. When the spiral is rotated slowly, it appears to come out from the center. When the rotator is stopped, the spiral gradually shrinks. This apparent movement is due to the terminal lag of the sensation.

Perception

53. Diagram of the optic apparatus. G (*Gesichtsfeld*) represents the field of vision; R, retina; P, primary centers for vision; and S (*Sehrinde*), visual cortex. Objects on the left side of the visual field stimulate the right side of the retina; those on the right, the left side of the retina. Note the manner in which the optic nerves cross, and the way in which they extend toward the cerebrum.

54. If we fixate upon c, it is seen as a single point; but a and b are seen as if they were each doubled. The diagram illustrates the manner in which we experience double images.

55. A typical chart for measurement of visual acuity. Cohn's chart is used to determine the visual acuity of small children who cannot read. The disk shows a design, resembling a letter, which is looked at from various distances. All the designs except one are covered by a second, superimposed disk. The child is given a rod with the design fastened to its tip, and is asked to duplicate the position of the design.

56. Hering's apparatus for testing visual depth perception. The subject has to decide whether the marble is dropped in front of, or behind, a fixed marble. Depth perception is much more accurate in binocular than in monocular vision.

57. Apparatus for demonstrating the law of identical lines of vision. Two sheets of plate glass are placed at a distance of about twenty inches apart, and the subject is asked to stand about twenty inches from the first glass. A fixation point (F_1) is indicated on the rear glass; then a small piece of red paper is affixed at S_1 and a green paper at S_2. Now a gray hue is seen at F_1. In the second test, the fixation point is indicated on the nearer glass, and the red and the green papers are located on the second glass. The fixation point (F_2) now appears gray.

58. A prism stereoscope, which is a device for production of tridimensional im-

ages. The photographs are taken with two cameras set as close together as the human eyes, and they are inserted at $m - o$. The observer now sees a tridimensional picture at c.

59. It appears as though all points on a moving wheel were going at the same rate; but, in actuality, the individual points on the rim describe cycloids.

60. Anschütz stroboscope, which is a primitive forerunner of modern cinematography. The apparatus consists of a drum with slits at equal intervals. The inner wall of the drum is lined with pictures showing different phases of a continuous movement. When seen through the slits of the revolving drum, the pictures seem to be in motion. This device requires the subject to use but one eye in order to secure the effect.

61. The auditory localization of stimuli. When the sound waves reach the ears simultaneously, the source is located as "straight ahead." When the sound waves reach the left ear (O_1, *Ohren*) before the other, the source is shifted to that side; likewise with sounds from the right side. Effective time differences for left or right localization can go as low as $1/30,000$th of a second.

62. Young's pseudophone. If the sound waves are reversed by this apparatus, the individual will be confused for a while, but he will eventually become habituated to acoustic orientation.

63. Aristotle's anomaly. If the fingers are crossed, and a pencil is moved back and forth at the crossing point a sense of being touched by two pencils will be experienced. The stimulus is perceived as though the fingers were in normal position.

64. The subject is asked to fold his hands in the manner shown in the picture, to look at his fingers, and to move quickly the one which is pointed out by the experimenter. Nearly always the subject will move the corresponding finger on the other hand. The illusion is attributable to the influence of habit. If the experimenter touches the subject finger, the error does not occur.

Gestalt qualities

65. One of the earliest problems investigated by *Gestaltists* is the analysis of factors producing and influencing visual space perception. Six laws are illustrated:

a, Proximity (Components of a configuration are integrated according to the principle of the shortest distance); *b, Similarity* (When there are several elements, there is a tendency to integrate similar elements into patterns); *c,* the *"Good" Gestalt Factor* (Elements which form a smooth curve tend to fit together); *d, Closure* (Lines forming unbroken boundaries of a plane surface are more readily perceived as a unit than are lines which do not touch); *e, Experience* (Habit influences the manner in which lines are brought into a configuration. Here a capital *E* is perceived.); and *f, Significant Resemblance* [*Prägnanz*] (Elements which do not deviate too greatly from the pattern are seen as part of the pattern. Thus the dots at the bottom are identified with the circle.)

66. Although the *Gestalt* is difficult to get, *b* is contained in *a*.

67. Can you see the square in this design?

68. Design and background. The white may be perceived as either the design or the background. However, symmetry favors the perception of the illustration as a design.

69. The small triangles are actually of the same degree of brightness, though *a* seems to be brighter than *b*. The explanation is that *a* impedes the closure of the *Gestalt* of a cross.

70. Design and background. Is it a white vase or two faces juxtaposed? The *Gestalts* alter quickly.

71. Is it a flight of stairs or a ceiling ornamentation?

72. Is it a six-pointed star or a group of cubes?

73. You see either four capital *T's* or a white design against a black ground.

74. Is it merely a jumble of black spots or the letters *I T A?*

75. At first, you see mounds; but look steadily at the picture. Do you see holes? Notice how the lighting-effect alters.

76. Is it a rabbit or a duck?

77. Do you see an old woman or a young girl?

78. Can you perceive him as looking upwards? downwards?

79.–80. **Double heads.** Rotate the book slowly by one hundred and eighty degrees. Notice how the first head vanishes and another takes its place. This effect is known as *transposability*. Mentally defective children seem to have trouble in perceiving any change.

"Psychology" of the hand

81. **The human and the gorilla hand.** One important difference is the fact that the human being is able to bring the thumb into opposition to the fingers.

82. "Hands" for specialized purposes: *a,* digging (mole); *b,* swimming (otter); *c,* climbing (sloth); *d,* running (horse); *e,* flying (bat). The human hand is not specialized; it is a universal tool.

83. In emotional states, there is a secretion of perspiration on the hands. This may be observed by smearing the hands with a small amount of iodine in castor oil, and then rubbing potato flour over them. Secretion of perspiration makes the flour turn brown.

84. The fact that many tools are, in a sense, models of the functions of the hand demonstrates its versatility.

85. Expressive hand gestures of a Hindu priest in Bali.

Memory

86. **The Ranschburg memory drum.** By means of this apparatus, the subject may be presented with various types of material to be memorized, the exposures being set at various time intervals.

87. Apparatus for measuring the reaction times for reproducing memorized lists, such as nonsense syllables. The subject speaks into the microphone on the left

the word which he associates with the one on the memory drum. The reaction time is recorded by the Hipp chronoscope, which measures time in one-thousandths of a second.

88. Mnemonics consist of systematic aids in acquiring and recalling knowledge. These pictures serve as a mnemonic device for learning the Morse code.

89. A program of a demonstration in lightning calculation by G. Rückle, one of the most famous experts in mental arithmetic.

Work and fatigue

90. The Mosso ergograph. The finger is inserted into a ring from which a cord runs to the weight (*Vikt*). The number and the strength of pulls are recorded on a kymograph (*Trumma*). By determining the total weight lifted (that is, the weight times the number of lifts) and the total height of all the liftings, the experimenter can express the results in foot-pounds or meter kilograms.

91. Two ergographs by the same subject. *A* was made when he was well rested, and *B,* after he had taken a long hike.

92. The hand dynamometer, an instrument for measuring the strength of grip. The maximum score is dependent upon psychological as well as physical factors. Competition, for instance, raises the score.

93. An esthesiometer, an instrument used to measure the two-point threshold. The points are applied singly and doubly, in random order and at various distances between the two points. Ability to judge "twoness" varies widely in different parts of the body. At one time it was thought that fatigue might be measured in terms of a dulling of this discriminative ability.

Emotions

94. Apparatus for recording the pulse rate. In general, pleasant experiences tend to quicken the rate; unpleasant experiences, to retard it.

95. Plethysmograph, apparatus for measuring changes in blood volume of a limb. The blood volume shifts to the skeletal muscles during strong emotion. This change is measured by having the subject insert his arm into a vessel of water, a rubber cuff keeping the water from running out. As the volume alters, a record is made by means of a stylus attached to a drum.

96. A respiration curve (*a*) and a pulse rhythm (*p*), *t* indicating the time line.

Symbolism

97. Each of these feathers had a different meaning for a tribe of North American Indians: *a*, the killing of an enemy; *b*, a scalping; *c*, beheading; *d*, the wounding of an enemy.

98. Indian symbols: *A*, war; *B*, morning; *C*, nothing; and *D*, eating.

99. Chinese ideograms: *E* (hands joined), full, complete; *F* (hands outstretched), acceptance, friendship; *G* (hands aloft), subordination, master; *H*(hands apart), removal, distance. These show how symbols pass from concrete to abstract meanings.

100. Egyptian hieroglyphics (also illustrating the transition from concrete to abstract symbolism): *A* (sun), division of time; *B* (writing utensils), writing; *C* (front of a lion), previous; *D* (wasp), royal dignity; *E* (tadpole), multitude; *F* (ostrich feather or any feather), fairness, impartiality; *G* (moon and stars), month; *H* (oral gesture), eating, drinking, speaking, thinking, knowing; *I* (ceiling), sky, superiority; *L* (water), cleansing; *M* (height), enthusiasm, joy; *N* (chieftain), dignity; *O* (child), education; *P* (mummy), embalming, rites, pictures, forms.

101. Transition from ideograms to phonetic symbols. *A* is a lute, but also *goodness,* owing to the likeness between the sound of the words. *B* is a scarab, but it means *to become. C*, a swallow, means *great*. In *D*, the first two symbols represent the sound of the word *bread;* next to them is the ideogram for *bread*.

102. These drawings were produced by children between eight and thirteen years of age when they were asked to symbolize words like *time, soul, New Year, light, dark,* and the like.

103. A pictorial record by North American Indians. Here is the message: Ten members of the Fish Tribe went in a canoe toward the mouth of a river. The lake is identified by the outline.

104. Picture writing by Alaskan Indians. The account is as follows: Fishermen left their boat (*a*) and sought refuge in a hut (*d*), where they have nothing (*b*) to eat (*c*). The message, on a piece of wood, was left in the hope that assistance would be given.

105. The Chinese ideograms for *Psychology*, composed of three parts which literally mean *heart, ways, study* (Read from top to bottom).

II. CHARACTEROLOGY AND TYPOLOGY

Facial expressions

106.–107. Facial muscles (after Hans Virchow). These are pictures of the muscles which are innervated in facial expressions.

108.–111. Piderit's analysis of facial expressions in feelings and emotions. According to him, expressions arose in the following manner: When tasting sweet, a person brings his jaws tightly together to get the maximum stimulation; when tasting bitter, he opens the jaws as widely as possible. Thus, the "sweet" and the "bitter" faces had their origin. Muscles about the eyes support the function of vision. Thereby, according to Piderit, sensory impressions and facial expressions were associated. At length, the facial expressions occur alone, without the sensory stimuli originally attached to them. In 108 there are the following expressions: (*a*) the sweet expression; (*b*) scrutiny; (*c*) sullenness; and (*d*) anger. In 109 these expressions are depicted: (*a*) contempt; (*b*) laughter; (*c*) boisterous mirth; (*d*) weeping. In 110 there are (*a*) the furtive look; (*b*) the charmed look; (*c*) concentration. In 111, (*a*) reveals sleepiness; (*b*) surprise; (*c*) bitterness; and (*d*) stark horror.

112. In the upper row are two photographs of a person expressing different emotions. These were cut in half and pasted together in the pictures in the lower row. It is evident that the mouth is more expressive than the eyes.

Physiognomy

113.–116. At one time the students of physiognomy, influenced by a writing attributed to Aristotle, held the theory that when human beings resembled animals they had the character traits of those animals.

16

117.–118. Humorists have satirized human types in pictures like these: 117, "The Poet;" 118, "The Introduction."

Phrenology

119.–120. Bissky's *electrodiagnoscopy*, which was a curious attempt to revive Gall's phrenology. The skull surface is divided into zones, each being identified with certain abilities and talents. The subject and the examiner both hold electrodes, and then the examiner touches the regions with his fingertips. The type and the intensity of the shocks are supposed to indicate the abilities and the talents of the subject.

Composite photography

121.–124. Francis Galton was the first to make composite photographs. These are produced by superimposing the photographs of members of the same trade or profession upon one another. Thus, the individual features become obliterated, and the features common to all members of the group are accentuated. 121, The ten most intelligent boys in a class of ten-year-olds. 122, The ten least intelligent. 123. Composite photograph of the most intelligent boys. 124. Composite photograph of the least intelligent boys.

Diet and facial expressions

125. Ten-year-old boys who lived on a vegetarian diet.

126. Twelve boys who ate meat.

127. Twelve girls who lived on a vegetarian diet.

128. Girls who ate meat.

129. Composite photograph of the boys who lived on a vegetarian diet.

130. Composite photograph of the boys who ate meat.

131. Composite photograph of the girls who had a vegetarian diet.

132. Composite photograph of the girls who ate meat.

133.–135. Thirteen-year-old boys and girls who lived on a vegetarian diet.

134.–136. Those who ate meat.

137.–139. Composite photograph of the vegetarians.

138.–140. Composite photograph of those who ate meat.

Facial asymmetries

141.–144. At the top of each set of pictures is a photograph of the subject. Below are synthetic photographs made by combining half the face with its mirror image. This has been done for the left and the right sides of each face. Symmetrical faces are rare. Some French people have developed the opinion that the right side of the face reveals the inner character (of a right-handed person), and the left half, the social nature.

Kretschmer's types

145. The asthenic bodily type associated with schizophrenia.

146. The face of a schizophrenic, revealing the asthenic type.

147. The pyknic build of the manic depressive.

148. The broad type of face associated with the pyknic build.

149. The athletic build.

150. The achievement type (Nordic).

151. The performer type (Mediterranean).

152. The destiny type (desert people).

153. The destiny type.

154. The salvation type (Near East).

155. The deliverance type (Turanian).

156. The deliverance type.

Rorschach and Szondi tests of personality

157.–160. These are the symmetrical inkblots included in the Rorschach test. Since they are chance forms, the subject's interpretations reveal his manner of approaching situations, his mental sets and attitudes, and his range of interests.

161. The Szondi test. The subject is asked to decide which faces he likes and which he dislikes. The photographs are of persons with such well-defined disorders as manic-depressive psychosis, paranoia, schizophrenia, hysteria, sadism, and the like.

III. DEVELOPMENTAL PSYCHOLOGY

Psychophysical development

162. Changes in the relative proportions of the human body from birth to age twenty-five.

163. Proportional changes in various parts of the body during maturation.

164. On the left, the skull of an infant one year of age; in the middle, of a ten-year-old child; and on the right, of an adult.

165. The grasping reflex, which is strong immediately after birth.

166. Graphic representations of how the infant spends its day. The segments signify, respectively, the following: (*a*) sleep; (*b*) sleepiness; (*c*) negative reaction; (*d*) feeding; (*e*) movement; (*f*) quiet wakefulness; (*g*) impulsive movements; (*h*) random play. Graph I shows the day of a newborn infant; II, of a three-months-old infant; III, of an infant five months old; and IV, of one who is twelve months old.

167. The respiratory and the brain-pulse (fontanelle) curves of an infant seven days old. The respiration curve is labeled *A;* brain pulse, *B;* time line, *C;* the mother's voice, *D.*

168. Effects of restraint of movement. The infant's head is held gently but firmly between the experimenter's hands; the infant responds with loud cries and struggling movements.

169. Stages in the development of posture, from the first to the tenth month of life.

170. Typical postures of a year-old infant. Responsiveness to various situations is depicted.

171. Fraternal (dizygotic) twins.

172. Identical (monozygotic) twins.

173. The "oral stage." The young infant explores the environment by putting objects into its mouth.

174. Defiance.

175. Christian Heinrich Heineken, a child prodigy. According to the story, he spoke High and Low German and Latin at the age of two; he is said to have had an extensive command of many fields of knowledge. He died at four years of age.

176. The manner in which children used to be dressed. At one time, children were considered to be miniature adults, and they wore adult clothing and wigs. Only the children of lower-class parents could enjoy the freedom of simpler dress.

Drawings by children

177. Drawings by very young children. It is interesting to note that the first drawings deal with human beings.

178. Development of observation and self-criticism as revealed by drawings; (a) by a child four years of age; (b) by a six-year-old; (c) at the age of eight; and (d) at ten years of age.

179. A house.

180. Animals: (a) dog; (b) hen; (c) and (d) horse; (e) pig; (f) dog; (g) pig. These drawings by young children are of interest because they indicate the fact that there is no one-to-one correspondence between the stimulus and the

response. The stimulus ("Draw a dog.") merely touches off the response patterns which the child is capable of making.

181. A child's drawings of a flower.

182. A tree.

183. Sketches of human beings in various situations.

184. A "social situation" as depicted by a young child.

185. Drawings by children of different mental-age levels: (a) by a boy whose chronological age was fourteen and whose intelligence quotient was 46; (b) by a boy aged nine, IQ 67; (c) by a girl aged eight, IQ 64; (d) by a girl aged five, IQ 77.

186. Sketch by an eight-year-old boy with pathological characteristics.

187. Drawing by a normal boy of eleven.

188. Drawing by a normal girl of eight: "Picnic."

189.–190. Drawings by the same girl: (189) "Newly-wed;" (190) "The Circus."

191. Drawings by a talented child at three years and five months of age. The grandfather and a great-uncle were artists. At a very early age, this child displayed enthusiasm for drawing, and attempted to draw profiles when he was three years and seven months of age. The sketch of a man (on the left) would rate at about the normal five-year level.

192. The drawings of a talented boy eight years of age.

193. Drawings of a talented boy nine years of age.

194. Sketches of a talented boy ten years of age.

195. A table, as drawn by three children.

196. A pyramid, as drawn by three children.

197. A six-sided pyramid on a cylinder, as drawn by an eight-year-old. These draw-

ings (195-197) illustrate the fact that children have no compulsion to produce a photographic likeness of the model.

198. Diverse reproductions of a model. Children were asked to draw the model at the top, with these results.

199. Drawings of a cone. Observe the diversity of representations, all of them made from the same model.

200. Drawings from the model of a cylinder. Each drawing was done by a different child, although all the children used the same model.

201. Drawings by Eskimo children.

202. Sketches by university students, who worked without a model.

203. Rock drawings by American Indians.

204. Cave drawings by Paleolithic man.

205. A reindeer engraved by a Paleolithic man.

206. Celtic alterations in designs of Greek coins.

207 through 209. Simple expressionistic drawings: (207) "Dream on a Boat," by Paul Klee; (208) "Animals in Captivity;" and (209) a sketch by Gabriele Münster. Note that non-representational or expressive art resembles the drawing of young children and primitive people.

210. Statuettes by young children.

211. Statuette by a young child. Five teeth are indicated in the mouth.

Montessori's methods

212. Material used by Madam Montessori for training the child to lace and button.

213. Material used for training muscular co-ordination. The cylinders are to be inserted into the proper holes.

214. A formboard for training in perception of spatial relationships.

215. Sandpaper letters used to give training preliminary to teaching the child how to write.

Measurement of intelligence

216. Which is the prettiest? (From the Binet-Simon Scale, age five).

217. Finding omissions in pictures. (Binet-Simon Scale, age seven).

218. Picture comprehension; the child being asked to tell what is going on in the picture. Very young children merely enumerate two or three details; later on they give a simple description; finally they interpret the scene.

219. The Gaussian curve. Intelligence, as well as many other traits, is distributed according to chance, with most scores piling up at the center and with relatively few scores at the extremes.

220. A device for demonstrations of chance distribution. Peas, dropped into the funnel at the top, are distributed according to the Gaussian curve. The observer has to infer the shape of the curve from the heights of the columns of peas.

221. An inference test. These pictures are shown one at a time, the child being asked to tell what is represented. The sooner the child is able to infer what the drawing represents, the higher his score.

222. A test for eidetic imagery. E. R. Jaensch tested children by having them look at a picture like this, and then describe it. He found that many young children have vivid images.

223. Materials for the mosaic test. Here the mosaics were simply thrown together by a mentally defective child of eight.

224. Mosaics arranged by a mental defective of nine years of age.

225. Mosaics by a normal child of eleven.

226. A ship made by a normal boy twelve years of age.

227. A mosaic by an intelligent girl of twelve.

228. The work of an artistic woman.

229. The work of a normal woman. Note that it is not chaotic, like the mosaics of mental defectives, but that it is not so good as some of the mosaics of normal children. Adults are sometimes inhibited by fear of criticism or by awareness of a lack of talent.

Personality appraisals

230. The well-organized "world" of a normal boy eight years of age. The materials are from the Build-a-World Game.

231. The "world" of a retarded boy ten years of age.

232 through 234. Pictograms by young children. The children were told to communicate with a foreigner, who did not know their language, inviting him for a visit, giving news about the family, and expressing good wishes: (232) by a seven-year-old boy; (233) by an eight-year-old girl; and (234) by a fifteen-year-old boy.

235. Examples of associations of young children: (a), (b), (c), (d), the manner in which a child imagined spatial relations among numbers; (e), (f) associations of spatial relationships among the months of the year; (g) the seasons; (h), the days of the week.

IV. PHYSICAL HANDICAPS

Deafness

236. Teaching deaf-mutes to recognize rhythms. The children place their fingertips on the piano while the teacher plays rhythms.

237. Speech instruction for the deaf. The instructor's voice is amplified, and the pupils sense the vibrations while they try to imitate the sound.

238.–239. Examples of gesture language. Note the general similarity among gestures of the Australian aborigine, the American Indian, and the deaf-mute.

Blindness

240. Learning to count.

241. Learning about animals. Note the happy expressions on the children's faces.

242. Part of the Braille system. When letters and figures are raised, the blind read by the touch method.

243. Miss Helen Keller, an American who became deaf and blind at eighteen months of age.

244. Teaching a child who is deaf, mute, and blind. The teacher helps the child to place the lips and the tongue into position for speech.

245. The manual alphabet, used by the deaf and by the deaf-blind.

246. A figure by Kleinhaus, the blind Tyrolean sculptor.

247. A bust by Schmidt, who is a blind German sculptor.

248. Bust by the blind Italian sculptor, Gonnelli.

249. A lion made by Vidal, a French artist, after he had lost his sight.

Art by the blind

250 through 253. Statuettes made by blind persons without talent. These are interesting because they reveal the type of concepts which the blind have. Note the huge hand of "The Beggar" (250). In 251, the blind person reveals his conception of terror. 252 is entitled "Deserted." In 253 — "The Dream of Jacob" — the ridges on the chest are intended to be expressive of Jacob's heartbeat.

Substitutions of feet for hands

254 through 256. Photographs of Unthan, an artist who was born handless.

257. A painter who had lost both arms holds the brush in his mouth.

258. The boy lost the use of his arms, and then learned to eat with his feet.

259. "Footwriting." It is interesting to observe that there are as many individual differences in writing done by the foot as in handwriting.

V. MEDICAL PSYCHOLOGY

Percussion

260. Apparatus for teaching percussion to medical students. Lead forms have been placed under the sheet of cardboard. Specimens of these forms are shown above.

261. Cardiac and pulmonary areas for percussion. First in the usual way, by auscultation and palpation; then only by the aid of the vibration sense.

Amputations

262. The stump illusion. After the loss of an arm or leg, the patient feels as if the limb were still intact. Gradually the "ghost limb" retracts into the stump. A patient who has lost an arm may eventually sense a "dwarf hand" in the stump.

263. Sauerbruch's operation. This consists of making a tunnel through the muscles of the arm, so that the artificial limb may be manipulated by the biceps (sometimes by the triceps as well). Facility in control is gained by exercises.

264. A patient who had undergone Sauerbruch's operation. He is being tested for the degree of control over the remaining musculature of the upper arm.

265. Positions of an artificial hand.

266 through 269. Representations of visions induced by mezcaline, a drug used by South American Indians during religious celebrations. Note the rhythmical characteristics of the visions.

270 through 273. Pictures drawn by a schizophrenic patient to illustrate his hallucinations. In 270, he depicts the frightful nature of some of his delusional-hallucinated states. In 271, he represents the hallucination of being in a mine, where a man's legs have been sliced into thin disks. Note the angle at which a miner is descending the ladder. In 272, he has the hallucination of being wheeled past the scene of a mass execution, while he hears the groans and cries of people who are being beheaded. In 273, the devil appears before him. The brass ball (center) is "the globe of the cosmos."

Hysteria

274. Characteristic posture (*arc-de-cercle*) of the hysteric.

275. Sketch by an hysteric to illustrate the two-fold nature of his personality: (*a*) his basic drives; and (*b*) the vigilant side of his personality, which watches lest these drives have a chance to express themselves.

276. An hysteric drew this picture while in the state of hypnosis. The heads are representations of childhood sweethearts; the animal is a goat or satyr; and the snake is an erotic symbol.

Drawings by the psychotic

277. An example of psychotic condensation. The sketch is supposed to depict a cellar, a tavern, a parlor, and a stable—all united into one.

278. An ink sketch by a paranoid schizophrenic. Note the repetition of designs, the absence of a general theme, and the careful attention to minute details.

279. Sketch by an art student with a manic-depressive psychosis, depressive type. His explanation of the picture: "A rolled-up salamander staring at a star, which is represented by the tear-shaped, sacciform organ (center) and the halo (upper left)." He adds, "I should like to turn my back to the world and to seek the Divine in my own Self."

280. A pictorial representation of a dream by a female patient. She explains the picture as follows: "I dreamed that I examined a neglected plant to find out whether the roots had died. Innumerable earthworms crawled out of the soil in the flower-pot. In the bottom of the pot was a small yellow snake, from which I shrank back in horror. It climbed out of the pot; and, as it came nearer to me, it grew larger and larger. The larger it grew, the less was I afraid of it. As soon as I saw that it wore a crown on its head I prostrated myself before it. The snake said to me, in a feminine voice, 'Now I must put you to sleep.' . . . I have found that by the act of painting this picture of my dream, and in particular, by surveying the finished work, I have awakened my mind to the symbolism of the snake. It is really the symbol of healing."

281. Another drawing by this female patient. The eagle is the symbol of the spiritual, of masculinity, and of the divine. The phallic symbol (lower center) is invested with the sublimity of lofty symbols. Both 280 and 281 are good examples of Freudian symbolisms.

Hypnotic phenomena

282. A hen in a cataleptic state. The hen was quickly grabbed and placed in this position, where it lay for some time.

283. A bear placed in a position of catalepsy, where it lay for a while as if transfixed by the gaze of the trainer.

284. Hypnotic analgesia. A tooth is being extracted while the patient is under hypnosis.

285. Hypnotic analgesia during a major operation.

286. Autohypnotic postures of a Yogi.

30

Art and phantasy

287-288. "War" and "Famine" as depicted by Kubin.

289. A drawing on an Attic vase (*circa* 500 B. C.) It depicts the departure of the soul from the body of a person just deceased.

Superstition, delusion, and schizophrenic symbolism

290. Natives of New Pomerania wearing cross-pieces in their noses to keep out disease.

291. Nose-stoppers fashioned by a psychotic to exclude hostile odors. It is of interest to observe that some psychiatrists have developed the theory of "archaic mentality" to account for resemblances such as those depicted in 292.

292. (*a*) Pipe tamper made by a psychotic; (*b*) figurine made by a native of New Guinea. Note the similarity.

293. Figurines made by primitive people: (*a*) by natives of New Mecklenburg; (*b*) by a native in West Africa.

294. Figurines made by a schizophrenic. Compare these with the figurines in 293.

295. (*a*) Figurines made by natives of the French Congo; (*b*) figurines made by a schizophrenic patient.

VI. OCCULT PHENOMENA

Dowsing

296. The divining rod. The dowser holds the rod lightly (top) and walks slowly around to locate the site for digging a well (center). When he discovers the site, the rod turns downwards. Dowsing is a very old custom which still flourishes in rural areas.

Chiromancy

297. The "meaning" of the hand: (1) will; (2) reason; (3) material Ego; (4) social Ego; (5) spiritual Ego; (6) objectivity; (7) art; (8) sensuality; (9) imagination and subconscious mentality; (10) social sense; (11) family obligation or responsibility; (12) consciousness and the Ego. Although systems of palmistry vary, they are alike in assuming that the hand reveals personality traits.

298. Hand-lines of George Bernard Shaw.

Mediums and séances

299. Willy Schneider, a well-known medium. He is wearing tights with phosphorescent stripes, so that his movements may be watched in the dark. It is curious that mediums cannot perform in bright daylight.

300.–301. Heads "produced" by the medium Eva C. It was later found that these heads were identical with pictures which had appeared in *Le Miroir,* a French magazine.

302. Margery, a well-known medium, "producing" fingerprints during a séance.

303. One of the fingerprints "produced" by Margery.

304. A writing-board used in séances. The "spirits" spell out the answers to questions on this board.

305. Chevreul's pendulum. The holder thinks hard of a straight line or a circle, and the pendulum swings in that direction. Occultists attribute the motions to spirit influences.

306. A diagram representing an occult philosophy of the significance of bodily proportions.

VII. APPLIED PSYCHOLOGY

Advertising

307 through 313. Examples of attempts to control behavior through advertisements.

Vocational tests

314. The sorting box. The pieces are to be sorted out and dropped through the slots in the box-lid. Performance is graded for speed and accuracy.

315. A formboard. The pieces on the left are to be arranged in the space at the right. The dotted lines do not appear in the test.

316. A test of visualization: (*a*) the designs are to be continued; (*b*) the other sides of each figure are to be adorned with the design now on one side (without turning the paper); (*c*) the cubes are to be counted.

317. A test of ability to visualize a complex motion. The direction of the lower gear-rack and the cog-wheel are to be described when the upper gear-rack is stationary, and the movements are to be described when the cog-wheel turns either to right or left.

318. Movements of the cog-wheels are to be described when the motor is rotated in either direction.

319. Rossolimo's test of concrete intelligence.

320. A cube-assembly test. The parts are to be fitted together to make a cube.

321. Giese's shunting test. The subject is required to shunt trains from one station to the other, according to the examiner's instructions.

322. A test of practical judgment. The subject is asked to tell what is wrong in this picture.

323. A test of scientific aptitude. The subject is required to describe what would happen when water enters at the bottom.

324. A wire-bending test. A (bottom center) is the model, and 1–5 are the results of attempts on the part of various persons to duplicate the design.

325. Blumenfeld's test for two-handed coördination. Crank handles, one held in either hand, turn the table and move a marker at a 90° angle to the movement of the table. The subject is asked to trace a series of curves.

326. A steadiness tester. The subject is given a stylus with which to trace various paths. A demerit is given when either side of the slit is touched.

327. A test for automobile drivers. The subject sits before the wheel and looks at a motion picture of traffic. He must steer the "car" through various situations, and "collisions" are registered on the apparatus.

VIII. ANIMAL PSYCHOLOGY

Brains of animals

328. Phylogenetic development of the cerebrum. The cerebrum is represented by the black areas. A is the brain of a shark; B, an amphibian; C, a reptile; and D, a mammal. Maintenance functions are controlled by the midbrain of these animals; in a general way, their capacity to profit from experience is indicated by the relative amount of cerebral development.

Animal learning

329. Maze for the study of learning by the earthworm. The worm is placed at A, and it makes either a right or left turn. If it turns right, it reaches the dark area (B); but if it goes to the left, it gets a shock (C-D). By a long process of trial and error, it learns to turn right.

330. A study of fish learning. The food is placed in a container of a given color and not in any of the other containers. Eventually, no matter what the order of the containers, the fish goes directly to the one which contains the food. It is believed that the fish discriminates among colors by their brightness.

331. A problem box for the study of animal learning. This type of experiment is frequently reported by American psychologists as a measure of learning capacity among animals. The hungry animal is placed in the box and food is put outside. By trial and error the animal releases the catch holding the door. After repeated trials, the animal opens the door right away.

36

332. A hen maze. The food is placed in one compartment and the hungry hen in another, with a glass plate blocking the direct route to the food. After repeated trials, the hen learns the maze. Then, even after the glass plate has been removed, the hen always goes to the food by the indirect route.

333. Diagram of a maze used in studies of animal learning by American psychologists. The animal learns the maze by trial and error.

334. Apparatus for studying the "homing instinct" of bees. The hive is mounted on wheels, so that it may be moved to various distances from its accustomed position. When the hive is moved, the bees fly directly to the spot where it formerly stood, and it takes them some time to discover its new location.

335. A plan for studying the auditory sensitivity of a dog. The animal is able to identify the source of sounds with amazing accuracy. Under favorable circumstances, the time difference between stimulation of both ears, followed by correct response, goes down to 1/30,000th of a second.

336. Clever Hans, a famous animal that could perform many amazing tricks.

337. One of the famous horses of Eberfeld. These horses were supposed to be able to read and to work problems in arithmetic. As a matter of fact, they responded to slight cues given by their trainer.

338. A blind horse that, allegedly, was able to answer questions traced on its skin. The horse answered by nods and pawings.

Expressive behavior

339. Expressions of a chimpanzee: (*a*) contentment; (*b*) grief; (*c*) laughter; (*d*) worry; (*e*) anger; and (*f*) excitement. Of course, there is a strong likelihood that the observer reads into these expressions his own interpretations.

340. Contrast between a young and an adult chimpanzee. The young animal looks more human than the older one.

Insight

341. The use of a tool by a chimpanzee. To get the bananas, the animal uses a twig.

342. An example of insight. The animal has piled up two boxes in an effort to reach the fruit. Not succeeding by this means, he has taken a stick with which to knock the fruit down. Köhler's famous experiments with chimpanzees are illustrated by 341 and 342.

Conditioned reflexes

343. Pavlov's technique for establishing a conditioned reflex. The hungry dog sees a red light flash behind the screen just before food is presented. The sight of food is the adequate stimulus to activate the salivary glands of the dog, and the red light is merely an attendant condition in the situation. Eventually, the flashing of the light will elicit a salivary response. The amount of salivary secretion is measured by means of a tube connecting a portion of the parotid gland to a recording device. Distractions interfere with the establishment of conditioned reflexes; hence the dog is fastened gently but firmly into position before the screen.

344. Sham-feeding. Pavlov's studies of the digestive functions were rewarded with the Nobel prize in medicine. Here is a picture of a hungry dog feeding. Although the food drops through a fistula in the dog's neck, the gastric secretions flow.

345. Yerkes, an American psychologist, utilized the conditioning technique in an experiment on the auditory sensations of the frog. As a rule, this animal does not respond to loud noises; hence some students had conjectured that the frog is indifferent to all sounds other than croakings. The pressure stimulus caused the frog's leg to twitch; but at the same time a bell was sounded. After repeated pressure-bell sequences, the experimenter was able to elicit a leg-twitch when the bell alone was the stimulus.

Drives

346. An *ephialtes* wasp plunges its stinger into the larva of a woodwasp.

347. An ant "milking" an aphid. According to older naturalists, ants "domesticate" the aphid, just as human beings keep cows, for their milk.

348. Nest-building behavior by an ant. Naturalists are not certain about the nature of such activities on the part of lower animals, but they no longer feel certain that the instinct-hypothesis is the answer to questions about this sort of activity.

349. Map showing the migratory behavior of the polar sea-swallow. Its breeding place (A) is about twenty thousand miles from its winter habitat (B).

350. The *charadrius dominicus* migrates regularly from the Sandwich Islands to Alaska, passing over about two thousand miles of ocean.

351. A map showing the distances to which trapped birds flew to get back home. After being trapped and marked, they were released in Berlin. The experimenter wished to learn how quickly they would fly back to their accustomed habitat.

352. Map showing the distance traversed by a dog to get back to its home. Twice the dog was transported about four hours flying-time from its home in Punchheim to the place marked A. Each time the dog found its way home, using the routes indicated on the map.

353. A map showing the pathways traveled by a dog in Munich to return home. Note that the second time it was taken to the area indicated in the upper right-hand corner of the map the dog came home by a more direct route. The assumption is that in some unexplained manner the dog benefited by experience.

PART TWO

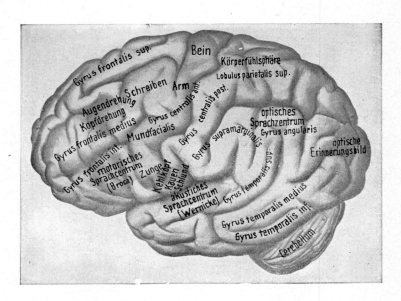

1

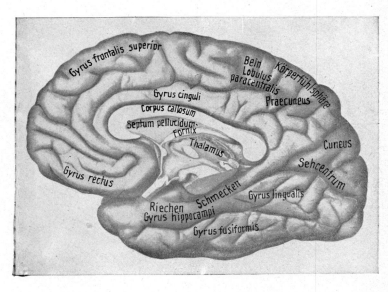

2

43

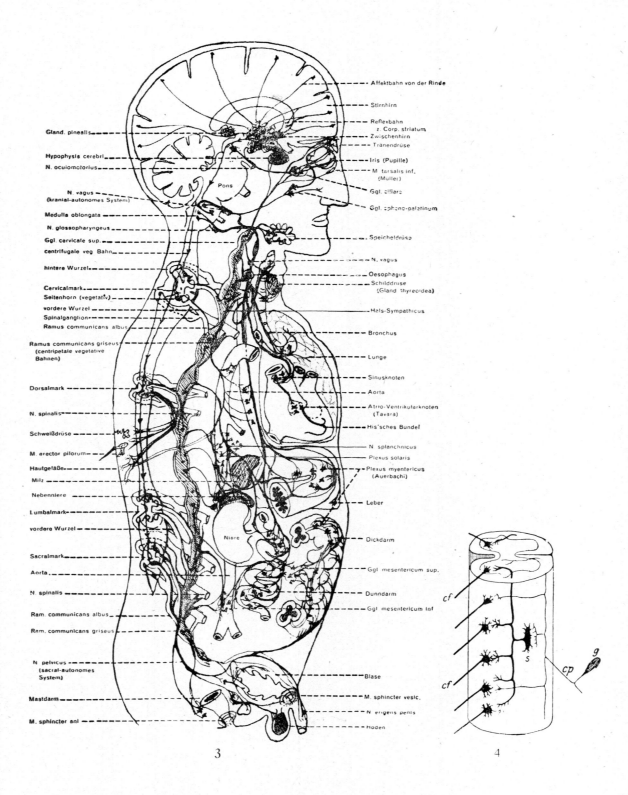

Affektbahn von der Rinde

Stirnhirn

Reflexbahn
z. Corp. striatum

Gland. pinealis

Zwischenhirn

Tränendrüse

Hypophysis cerebri

Iris (Pupille)

N. oculomotorius

M. tarsalis inf.
(Müller)

N. vagus
(kranial-autonomes System)

Ggl. ciliare

Ggl. spheno-palatinum

Medulla oblongata

N. glossopharyngeus

Speicheldrüse

Ggl. cervicale sup.

centrifugale veg Bahn

N. vagus

hintere Wurzel

Oesophagus

Schilddrüse
(Gland. thyreoidea)

Cervicalmark

Seitenhorn (vegetativ)

Hals-Sympathicus

vordere Wurzel

Spinalganglion

Ramus communicans albus

Bronchus

Ramus communicans griseus
(centripetale vegetative
Bahnen)

Lunge

Sinusknoten

Dorsalmark

Aorta

N. spinalis

Atrio-Ventrikularknoten
(Tavara)

Schweißdrüse

His'sches Bundel

M. erector pilorum

N. splanchnicus

Plexus solaris

Hautgefäße

Plexus myentericus
(Auerbachi)

Milz

Nebenniere

Leber

Lumbalmark

vordere Wurzel

Dickdarm

Sacralmark

Aorta

Ggl. mesentericum sup.

N. spinalis

Dunndarm

Ram. communicans albus

Ggl. mesentericum inf

Ram. communicans griseus

N. pelvicus
(sacral-autonomes
System)

Blase

Mastdarm

M. sphincter vesic.

N. erigens penis

M. sphincter ani

Hoden

cf

s

g

cf

cp

3

4

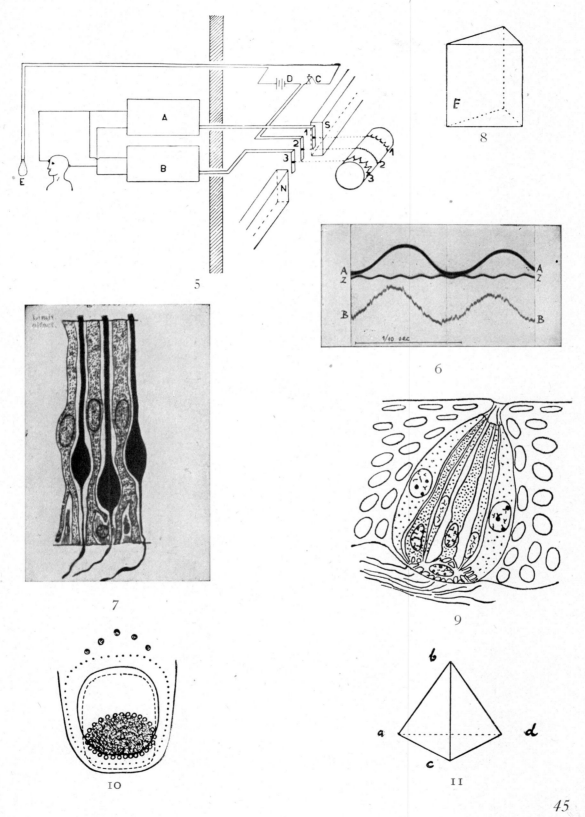

5

8

6

1/10 sec

7

9

10

II

45

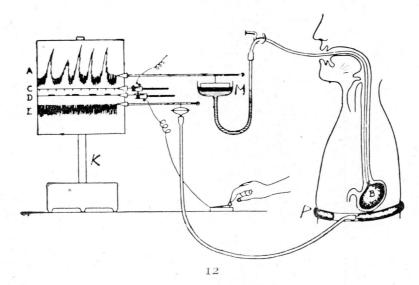

12

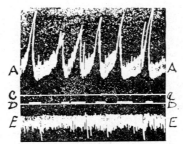

13

14

15

46

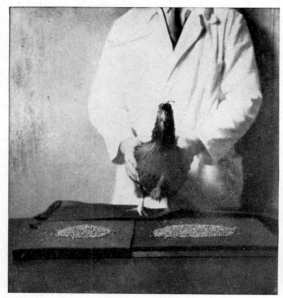

16

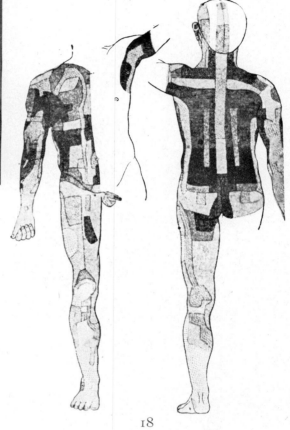

18

17

47

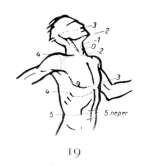

19

20

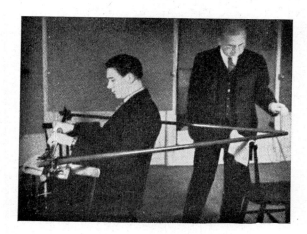

21

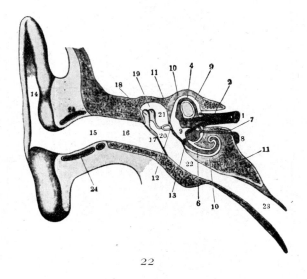

22

48

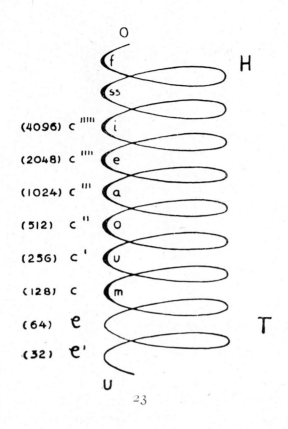

O

f

H

ss

(4096) c""" i

(2048) c"" e

(1024) c"' a

(512) c" o

(256) c' u

(128) c m

(64) e

T

(32) e'

U

23

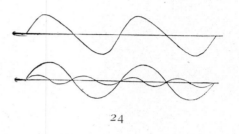

24

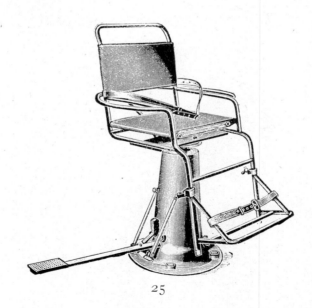

25

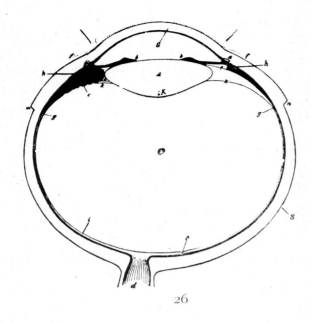

26

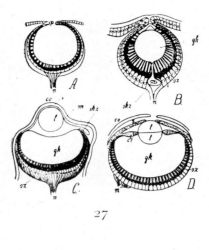

27

28

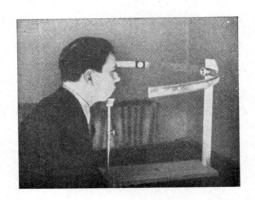

29

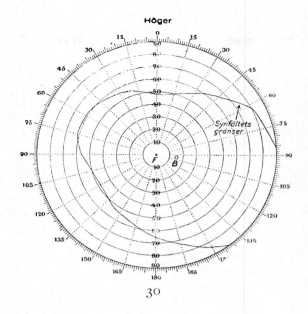

Höger

30

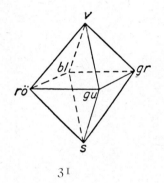

31

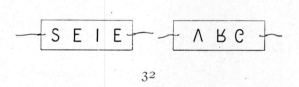

32

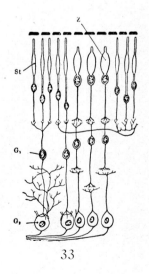

33

51

34

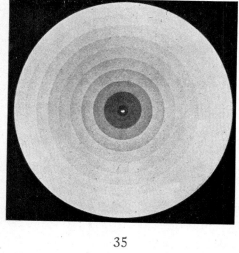

35

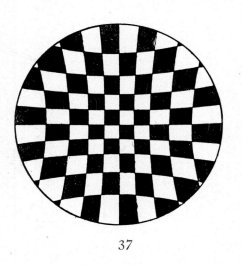

36

37

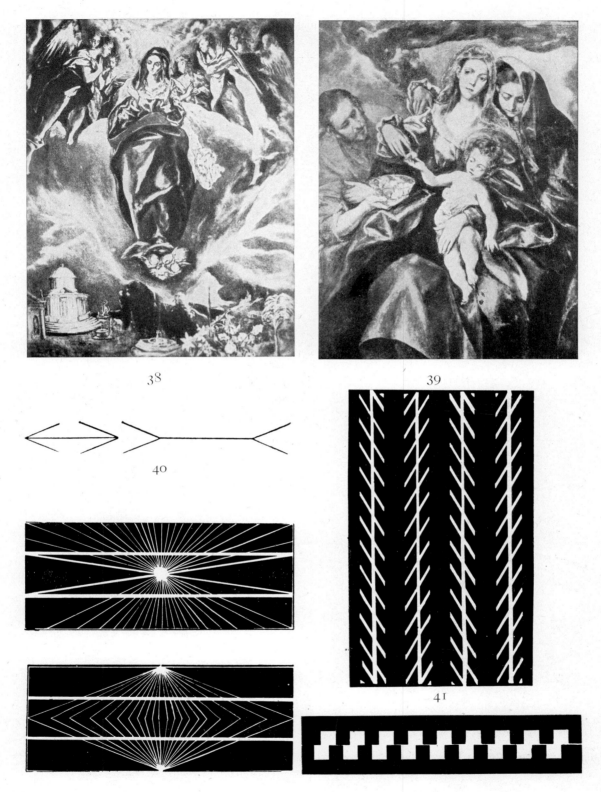

38

39

40

41

42

43

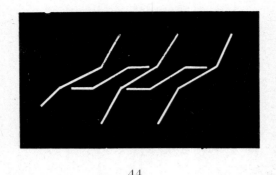

44

45

46

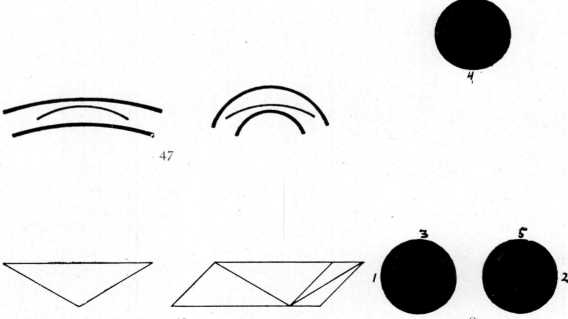

47

49

48

54

51

50

52

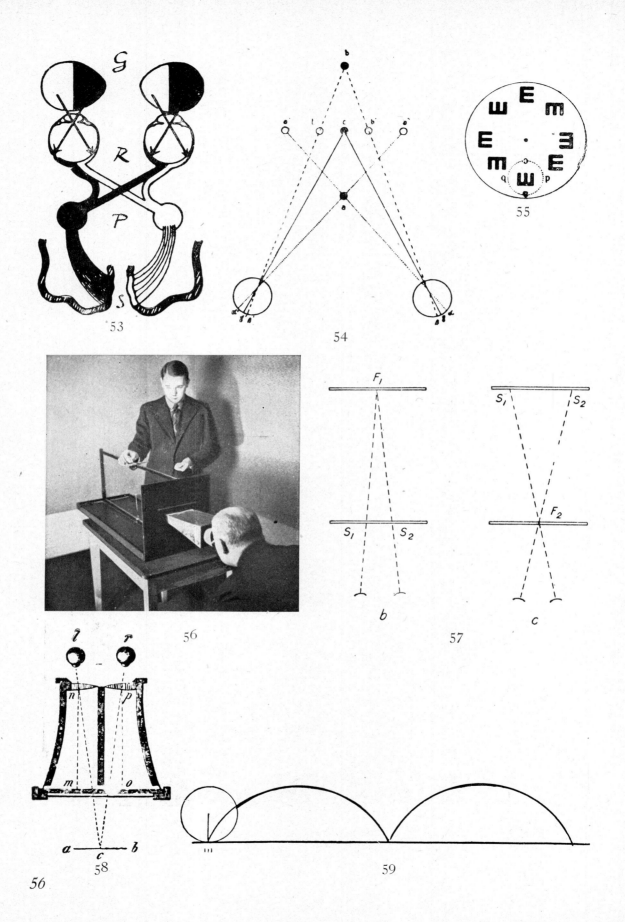

53

54

55

56

57

b

c

58

59

56

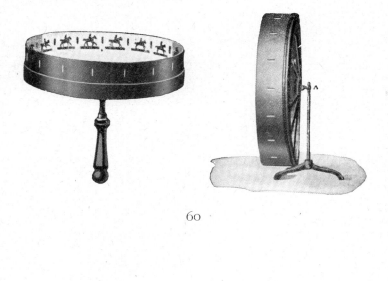

60

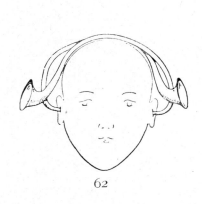

61

62

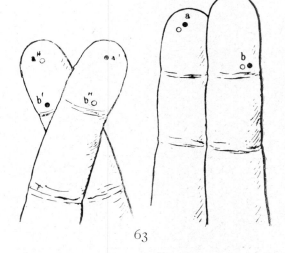

63

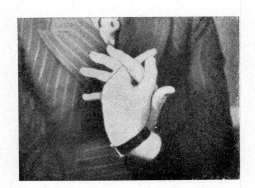

64

57

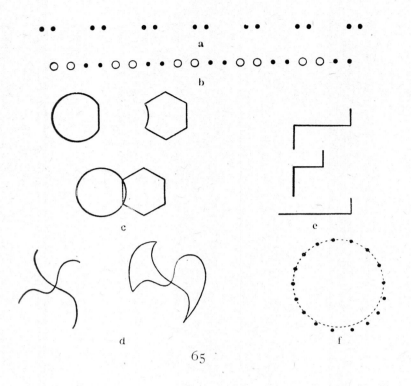

a

b

c

d

e

f

65

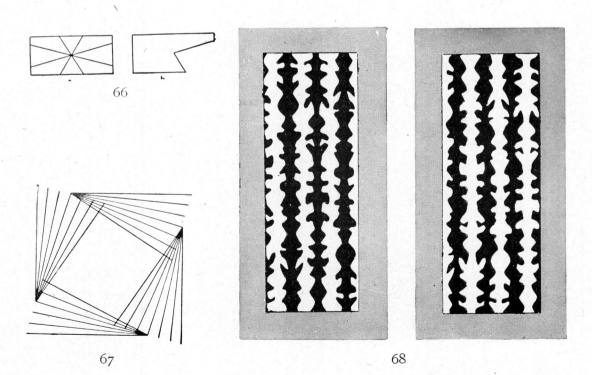

66

67

68

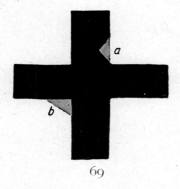

69

70

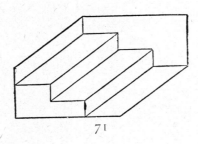

71

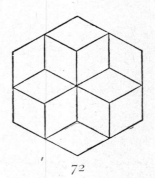

72

73

74

59

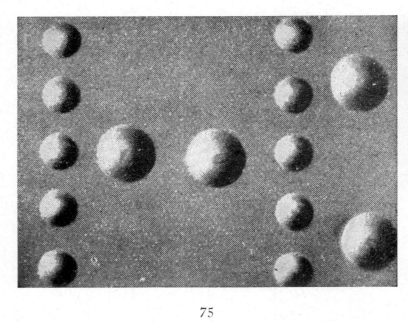

75

76

78

77

79

80

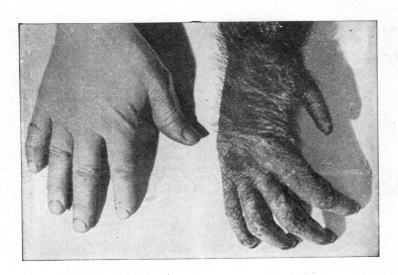

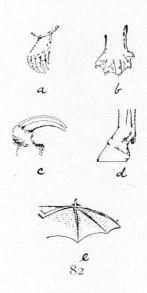

81

82

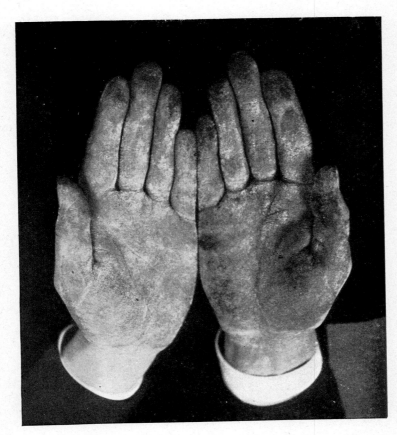

83

61

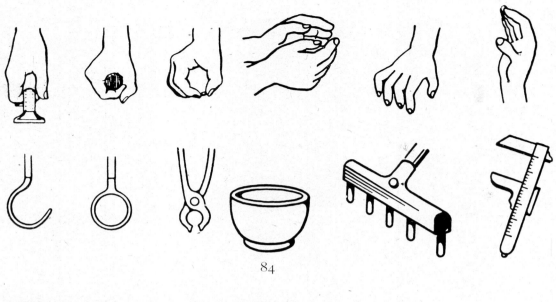

84

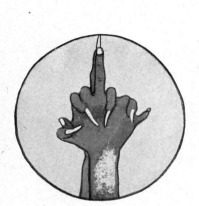

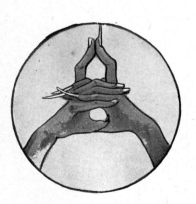

85

86

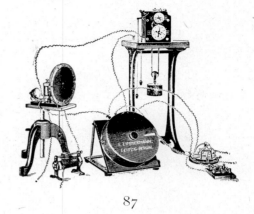

87

88

63

Experimental-Vortrag:
Dr. phil. G. Rückle

der unerreichte Meister der Rechenkunst

Alle Aufgaben werden im Kopfe ohne Niederschreiben der Zahlen gelöst.

Das geehrte Publikum wird höflichst gebeten, eine möglichst große Anzahl vorher berechneter Aufgaben stellen und die Lösungen auf die Richtigkeit prüfen zu wollen.

PROGRAMM:

I.

1. Gedächtnisversuch mit einem Karree von 49 Ziffern, die einmal vom Publikum genannt werden.

2. Erheben von Zahlen unter 100 zur 3. und 4. Potenz. Beispiele:
$$87^3 = 87 \times 87 \times 87 = ?$$
$$79^4 = 79 \times 79 \times 79 \times 79 = ?$$

3. Quadrate 3- und 4stell. Zahlen, Beisp.: 437×437 ? 7642×7642 ?

4. Ausziehen der Quadratwurzel aus 6- bis 8stelligen Zahlen mit Angabe des Restes.

5. Multiplikation verschiedener 3stell. Zahlen. Beisp.: 683×869 ?

6. Ausziehen der Kubikwurzel aus 6stell. Zahlen mit Angabe des Restes.

7. Zerlegung 5- bis oder 6stelliger Zahlen in die Summe von 3 bis 4 Quadratzahlen. Beispiel:

$$89519 = 293^2 + 57^2 + 15^2 + 14^2$$

```
           85849
            3249
             225
             196
          _____
           89519
```

8. Multiplikation 5stell. mit 3stell. Zahlen. Beispiel: 58327×674 ?

9. Multiplikation beliebiger 4stell. Zahlen. Beispiel: 5238×7387 ?

10. Fünfte und sechste Potenz 2stell. Zahlen. Beispiele:
$$97^5 = 97 \times 97 \times 97 \times 97 \times 97 = ?$$
$$82^6 = 82 \times 82 \times 82 \times 82 \times 82 \times 82 = ?$$

II.

1. Gedächtnisversuche mit einer 72stell. Zahl, die in 6stell. Zahlen vom Publikum genannt wird.

2. Dritte und vierte Potenz 3stell. Zahlen. Beispiele:
$$541^3 = 541 \times 541 \times 541 = ?$$
$$768^4 = 768 \times 768 \times 768 \times 768 = ?$$

3. Quadrate 5- und 6 stelliger Zahlen. Beispiele:
$$89376^2 = 89376 \times 89376 = ?$$
$$257895^2 = 257895 \times 257895 = ?$$

4. Dritte Wurzel aus aufgehenden 6- bis 12 stelligen Zahlen.

5. Fünfte, sechste und höhere Wurzel aus 6- bis 18 stelligen Zahlen.

6. Gleichzeitiges Rechnen und Auswendiglernen. Eine 4stell. Zahl wird quadriert (mit sich selbst multipliziert), während eine 24 stellige, während des Rechnens vorgelesene Zahl auswendig gelernt wird.

7. Berechnen von Numerus und Logarithmus beliebiger Zahlen im Kopf.

8. Ausziehen von 10. bis 20. Wurzel aus 20- bis 40 stell. Zahlen.

9. Zinseszins- und Rentenrechnung.

10. Berechnung von Kreisumfang und Kreisfläche, von Kugeloberfläche und Kugelinhalt.

Programm 10 Pfg.

89

64

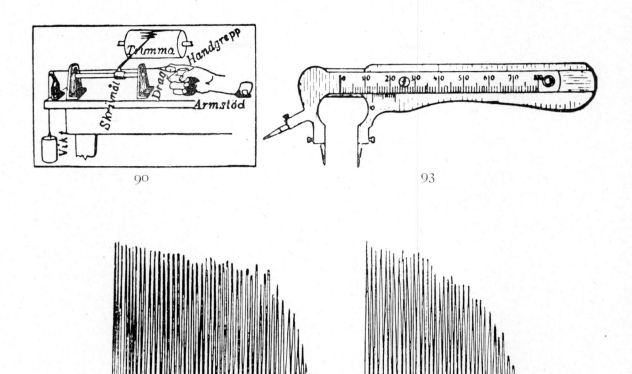

90

93

A   B

91

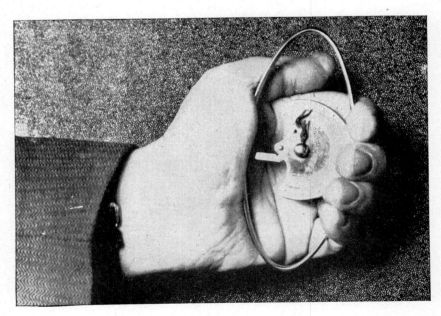

92

65

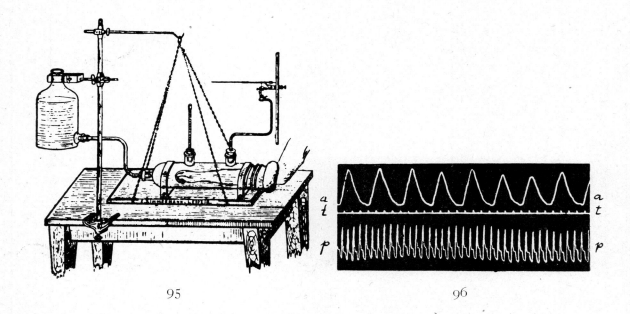

95

96

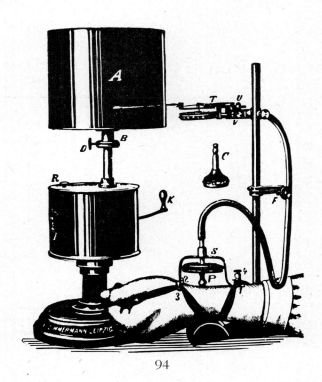

94

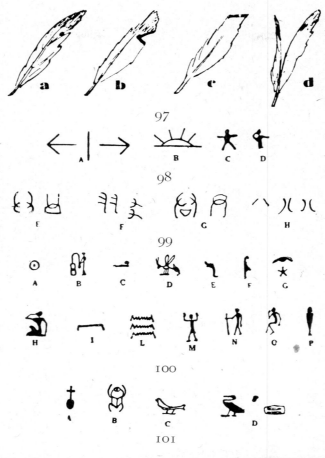

97

98

99

100

101

102

103

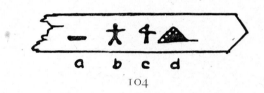

a b c d

104

心 "Heart," mind

理 "Ways"

學 "Study'

105

68

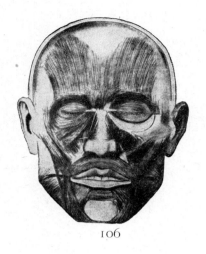

106

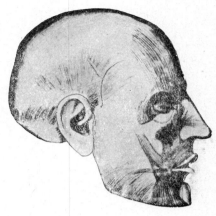

107

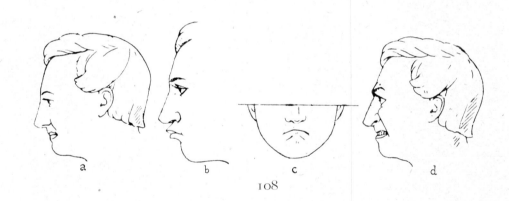

a   b   c   d

108

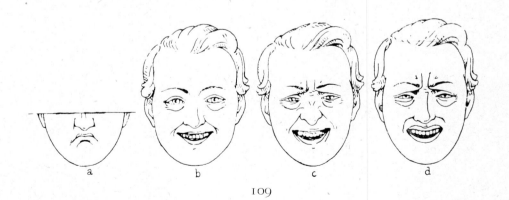

a   b   c   d

109

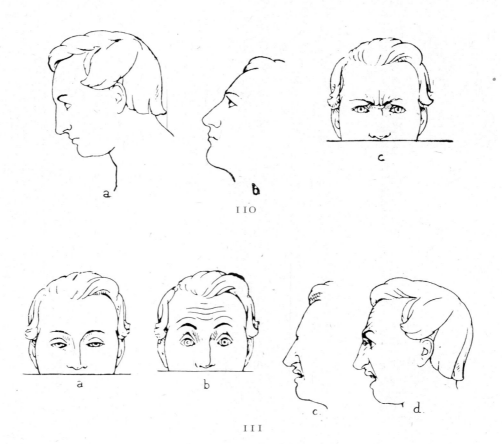

110

111

112

70

113

114

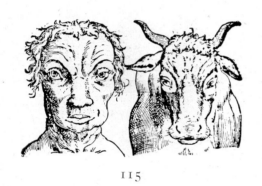

115

116

117

118

71

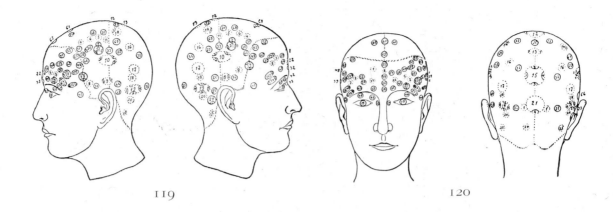

119　　　　　　　　　　　　120

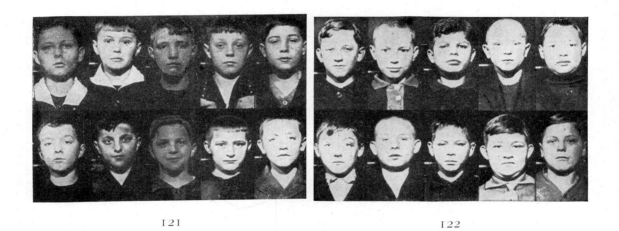

121　　　　　　　　　　　　122

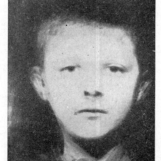

123　　　　　　　　　　　　124

72

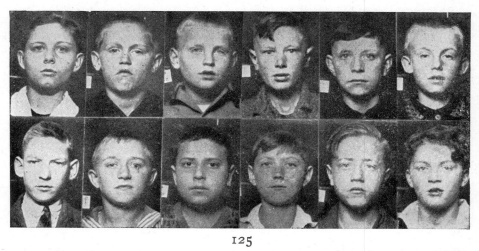

125

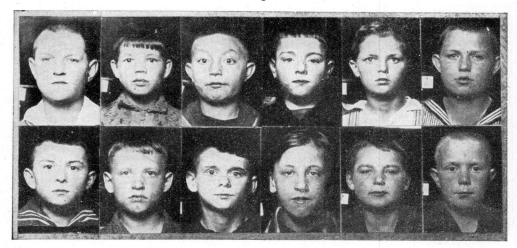

126

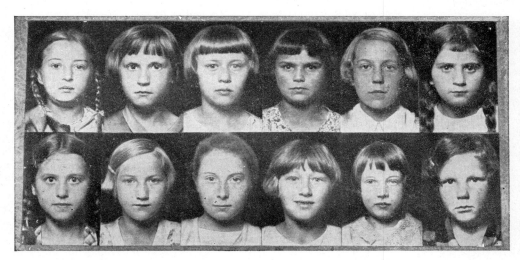

127

73

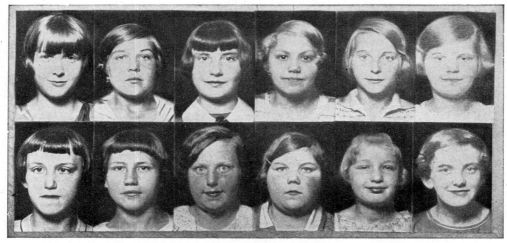

128

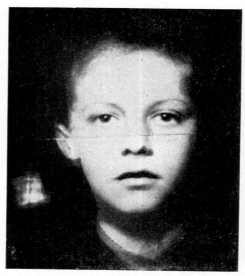

129

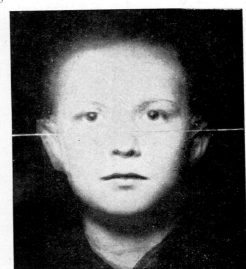

130

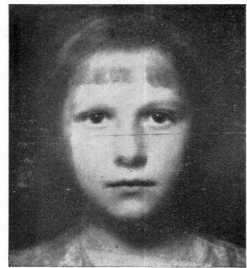

131

132

74

133

135

134

136

137

138

139

140

141

142

143

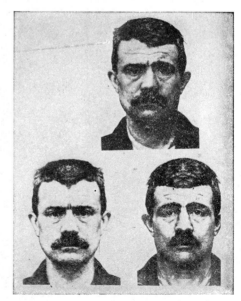

144

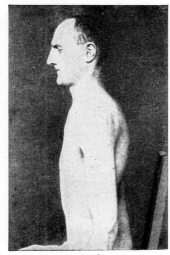

145

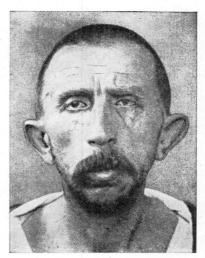

146

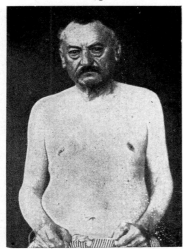

147

148

149

77

150

151

152

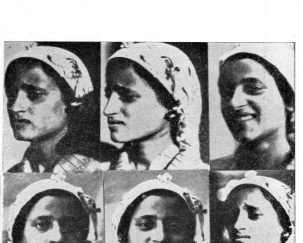

153

154

155

156

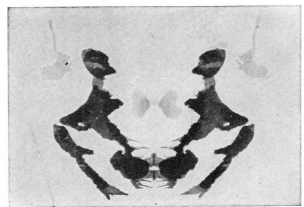

157

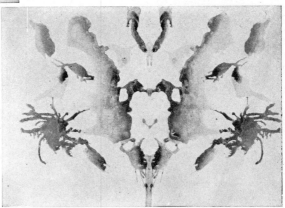

158

159

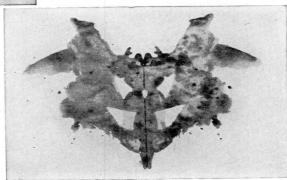

160

79

161

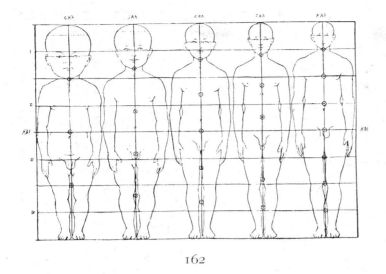

162

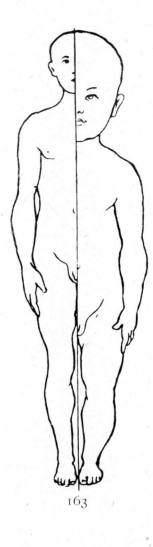

163

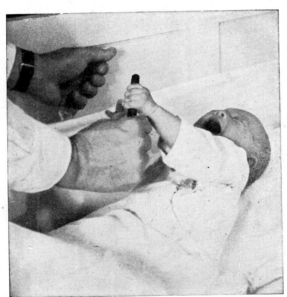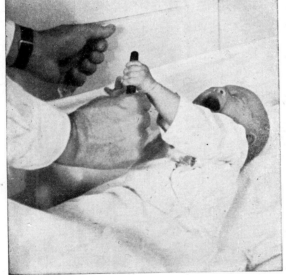

165

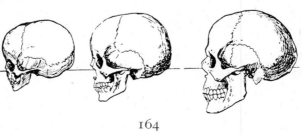

164

81

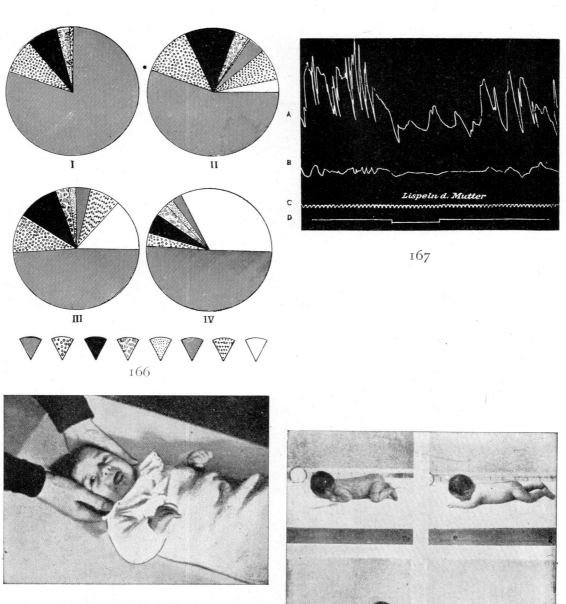

I   II

III   IV

166

Lispeln d. Mutter

167

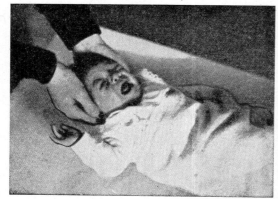

168

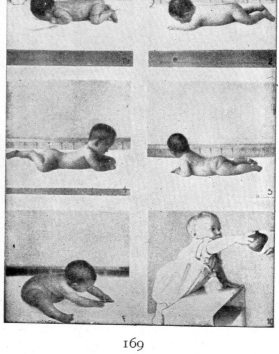

169

82

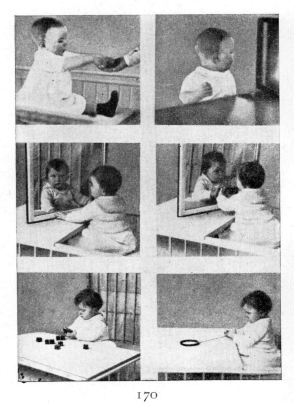

172

170

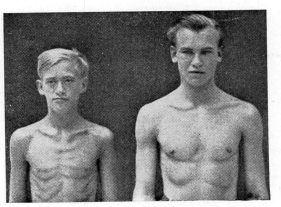

171

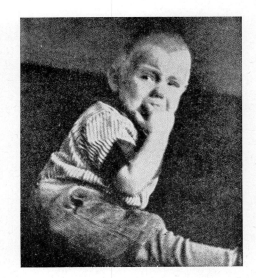

173

Kind, deßen gleichen nie vorhin ein Tag gebahr!
Die Nach-Welt wird Dich zwar mit ewgem Schmuck umlauben;
Doch auch nur kleinen Theils Dein großes Wißen glauben,
Das dem, der Dich gekannt, selbst unbegreiflich war.

175

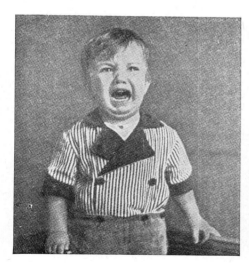

174   176

177

a.   b.   c.   d.

178

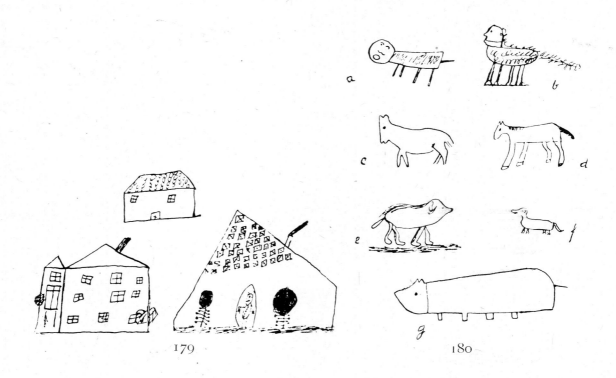

179

180

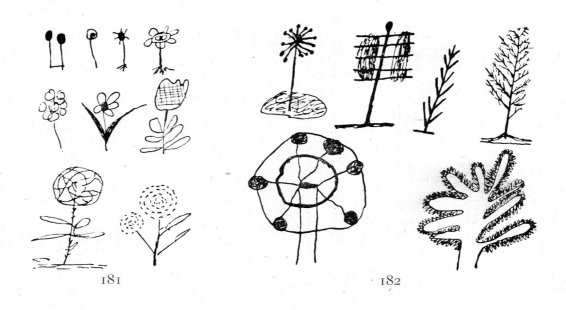

181

182

184

183

186

185

187

188

189

190

191

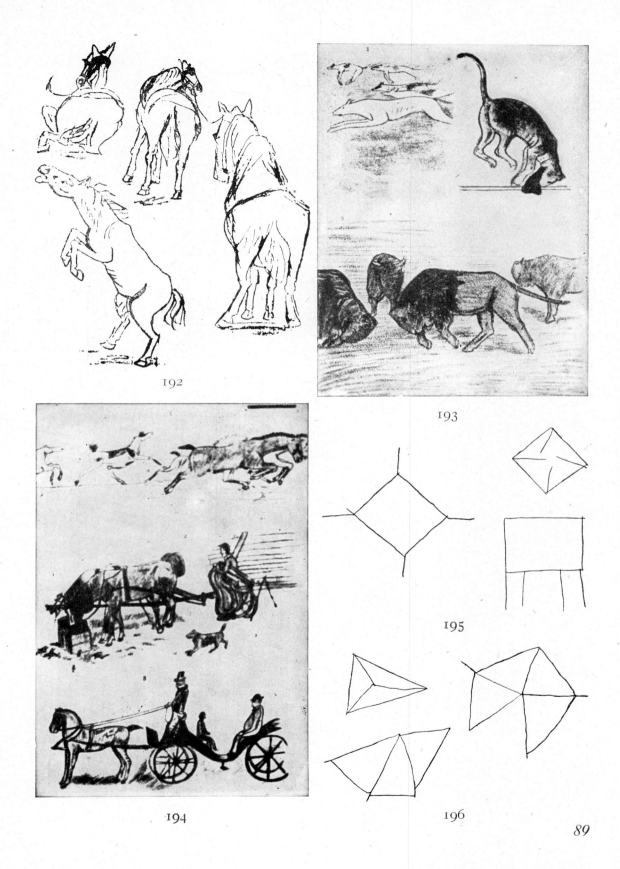

192

193

194

195

196

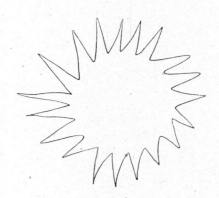

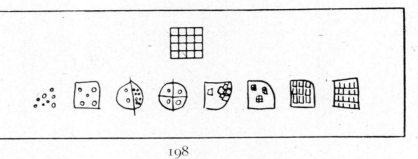

198

199

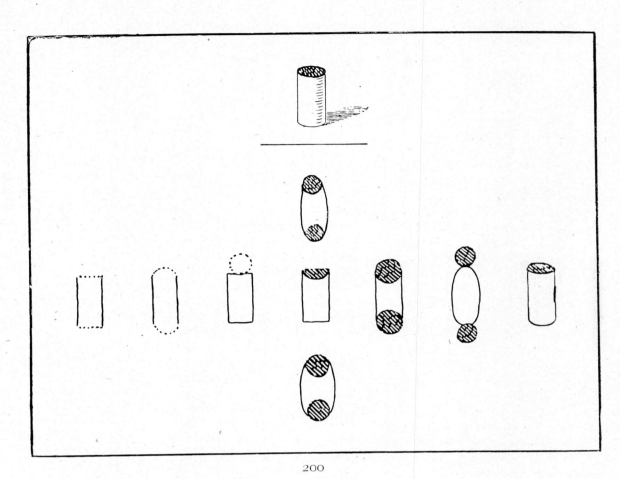

200

201

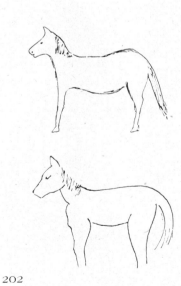

202

91

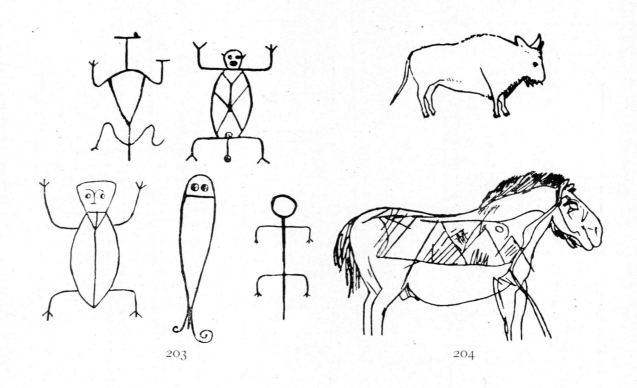

203

204

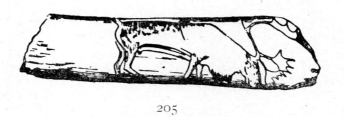

205

a   b   c

206

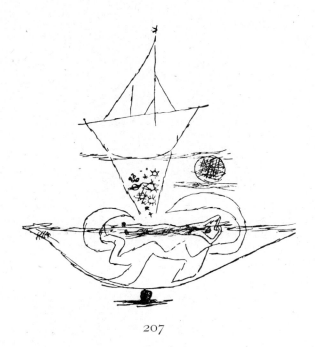

207

209

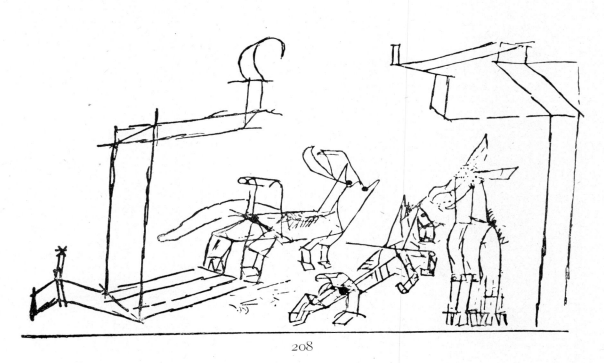

208

93

210

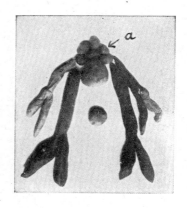

211

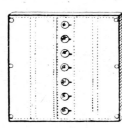 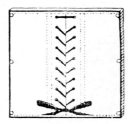

212

213

214

215

216

217

218

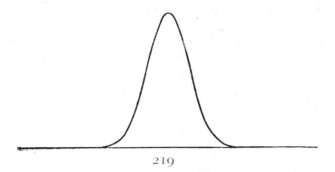

219

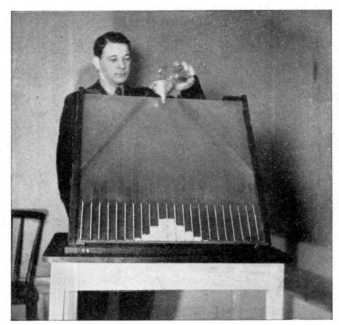

220

I

II

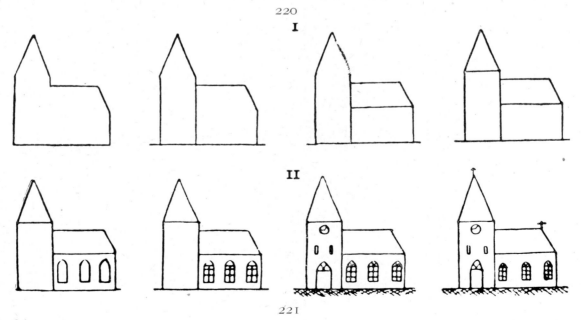

221

222

223

224

97

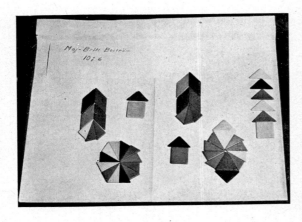

225

226

227

228

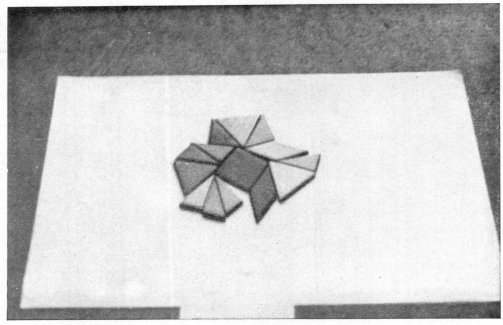

229

230

231

99

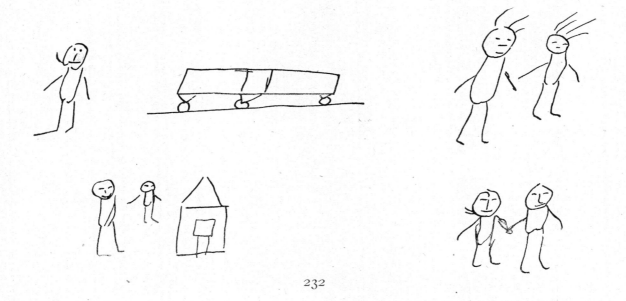

232

233

234

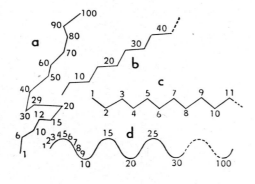

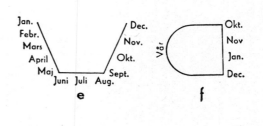

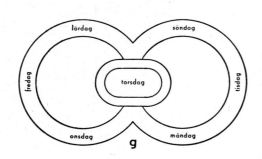

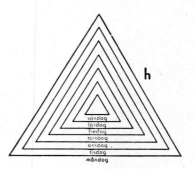

235

236

A	B	C
AUSTRALIAN	RED INDIAN	DEAF MUTE
COME (HITHER)	COME	COME
GO (THITHER)	GO	GO
QUESTION Alternative: Shrug arms & shoulders	QUESTION	QUESTION (= position uncertain)
YES	YES	YES
NO (Reject with palm of hand)	NO (Reject with back of hand & return to original position)	NO (As in R.I. sign)

238

237

AUSTRALIAN	RED INDIAN.	DEAF MUTE.
BULLOCK	BUFFALO	HORNED CATTLE
BIRD (Flapping wings)	BIRD (Flapping wings)	BIRD (Flapping Wings)
DIVING BIRD (Small Hawk)	HAWk	DIVING BIRD Sign for BIRD (see above) and
SNAKE	SNAKE	SNAKE
FROG	FROG	FROG
HUT	TEPPEE	HOUSE vertical walls may also be indicated

239

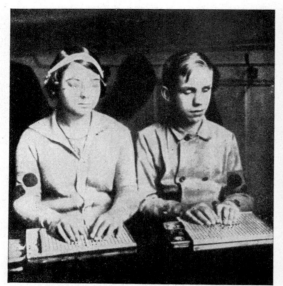

240

241

242

243

244

245

247

246

248

249

250

251

252

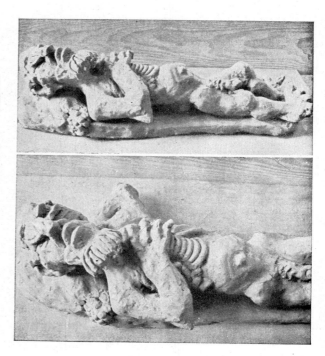

253

254

255

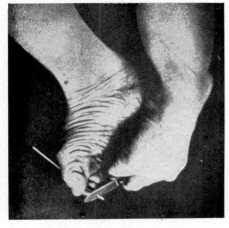

256

257

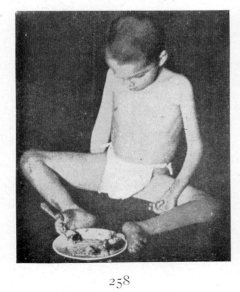

258

259

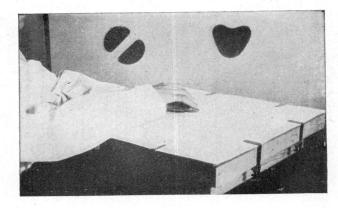

260

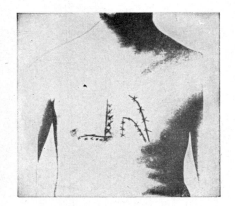

261

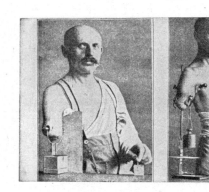

263

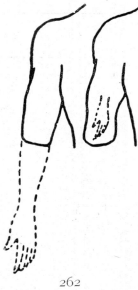

262

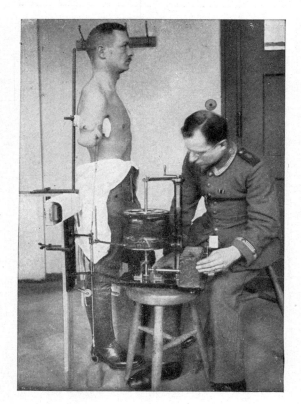

264

265

274

275

276

277

278

279

280

281

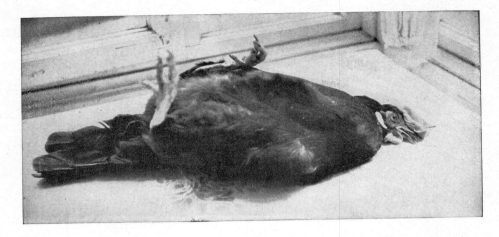

282

283

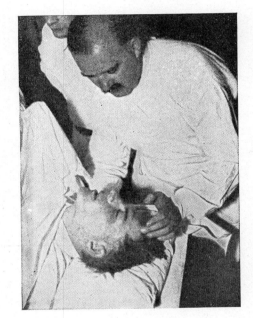

285

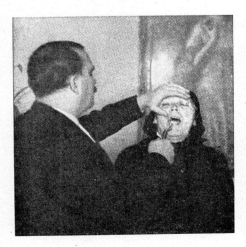

284

286

287

288

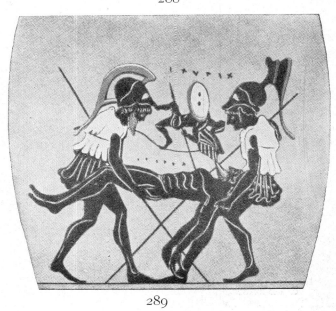

289

290

291

292

293

294

295

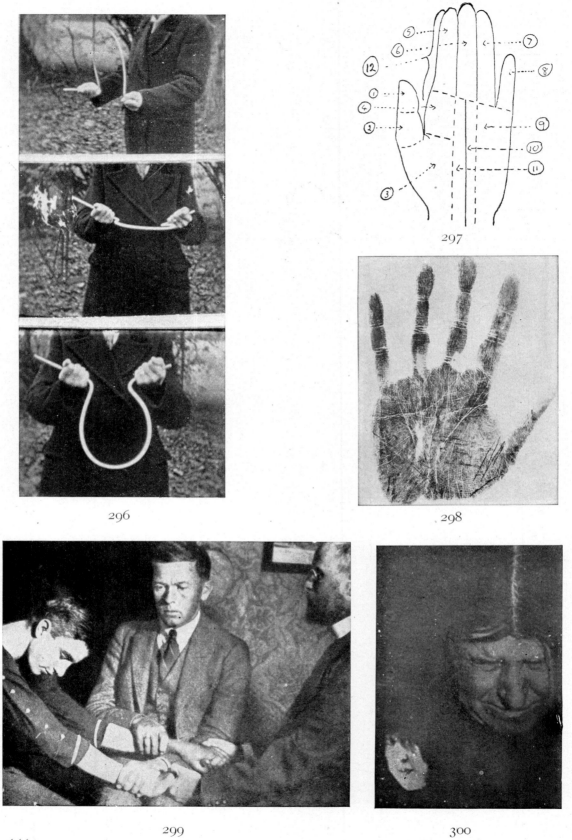

296

297

298

299

300

301

302

303

304

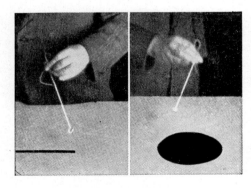

305

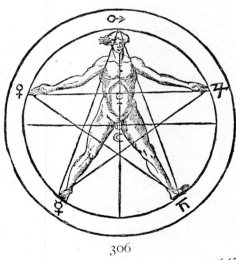

306

307

308

309

310

311

THE MAN WHO COUGHED
AS THE COLONEL SIGHTED HIS FIRST GROUSE

The MILD cigarette would have saved him

312

The MILD cigarette would have saved him . . .

The man who coughed at the Croquet Championship

313

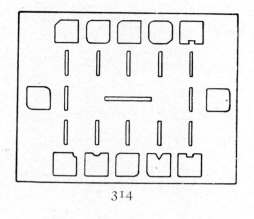

314

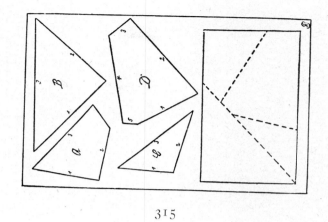

315

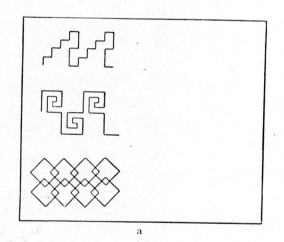

a

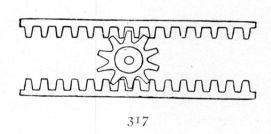

317

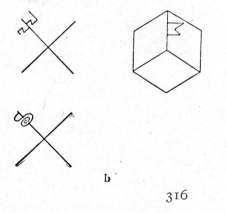

b

316

c

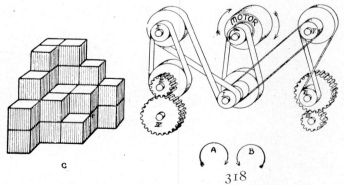

318

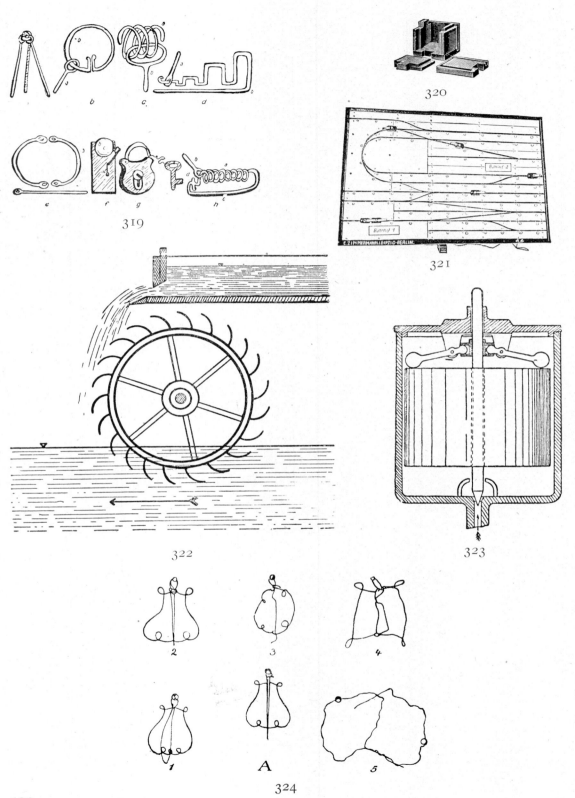

319

320

321

322

323

2

3

4

1

A

5

324

325

326

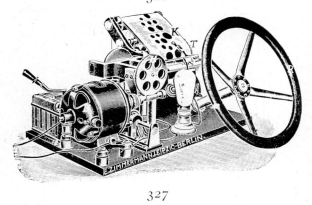

327

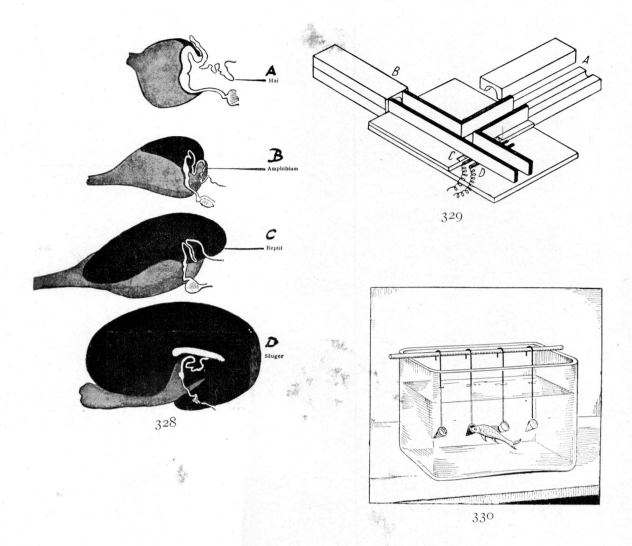

A — Hai

B — Amphibium

C — Reptil

D — Säuger

328

329

330

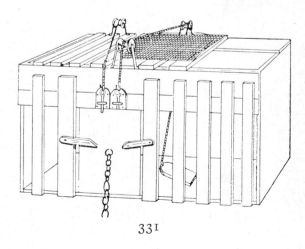

331

332

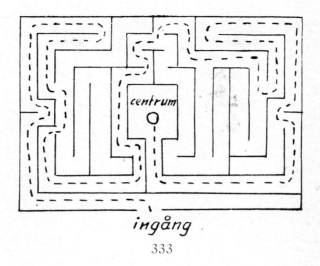

centrum

ingång

333

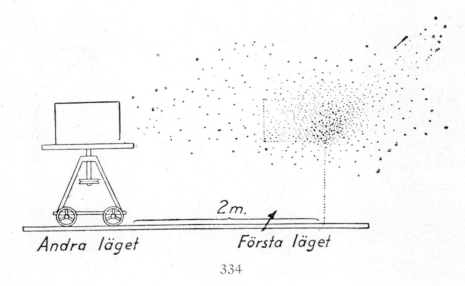

2 m.

Andra läget

Första läget

334

335

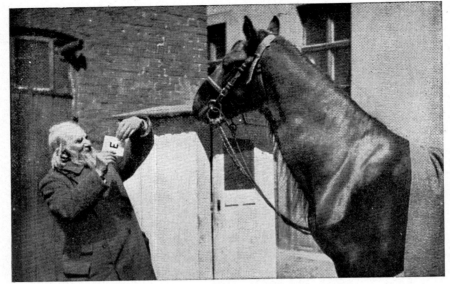

336

337

338

124

339

340

341

342

343

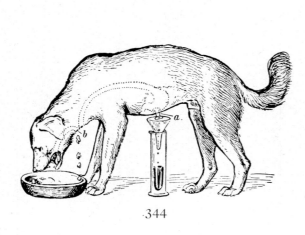

344

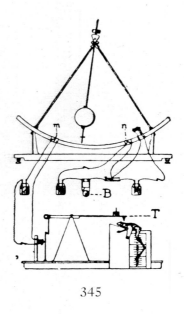

345

346

347

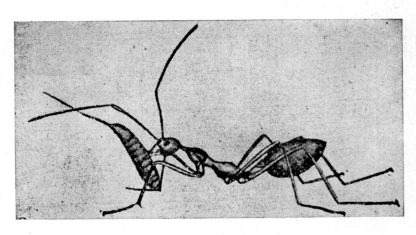

348

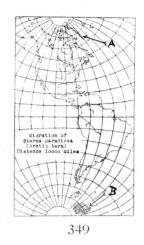

349

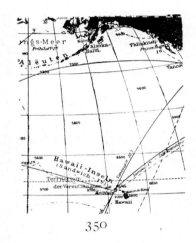

350

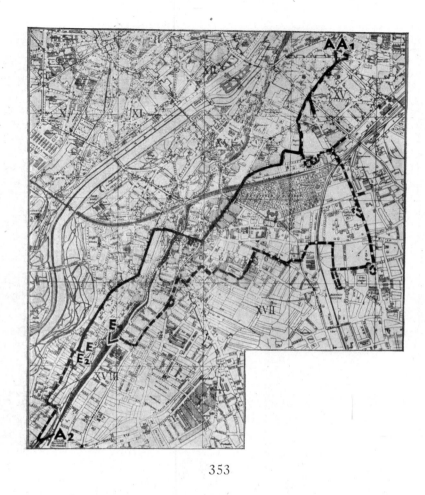

353

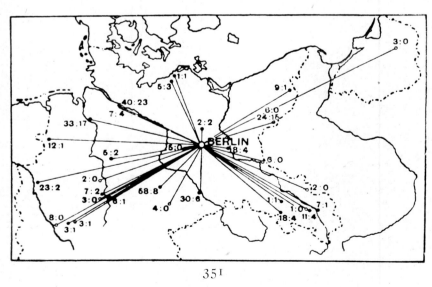

351

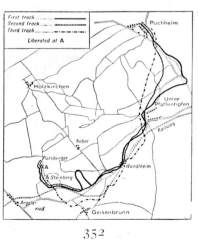

352

128

IX. EMINENT PSYCHOLOGISTS

354. A. Adler (1870—1937). Austria and the United States. Founder of Individual Psychology.

355. F. C. Bartlett (1886—   ). England. Experimental and social psychology.

356. W. M. Bechterew (1857—1925). Russia. Reflexology.

357. A. Binet (1857—1911). France. Intelligence measurement.

358. E. G. Boring (1886—   ). United States. Experimental psychology.

359. B. Bourdon (1860—   ). France. Experimental psychology.

360. C. Burt (1883—   ). England. Educational and experimental psychology.

361. E. Claparède (1873—1940). Switzerland. Child and educational psychology.

362. J. Drever (1873—   ). Scotland. Experimental psychology.

363. G. T. Fechner (1801—1887). Germany. Founder of psychophysics.

364. J. C. Flugel (1884—   ). England. Experimental psychology and psychoanalysis.

365. S. Freud (1856—1939). Austria and England. Founder of Psychoanalysis.

366. F. Galton (1882—1911). England. Experimental psychology and individual differences.

367. A. L. Gesell (1880—   ). United States. Child psychology.

368. A. E. Gemelli (1878—   ) Italy. Experimental psychology.

369. H. von Helmholtz (1821—1894). Germany. Physics, physiological psychology, and psychophysics.

370. E. Hering (1834—1918). Germany. Physiological psychology.

371. G. Heymans (1857—1930). Netherlands. Philosophical and experimental psychology.

372. W. S. Hunter (1889—   ). United States. Experimental and animal psychology.

373. H. Höffding (1843—1931). D e n m a r k. Philosophical psychology.

374. P. Janet (1858—1947). France. Psychiatry and psychology.

375. C. G. Jung (1875—1947). Switzerland. Founder of Analytic Psychology.

376. K. Koffka (1886—1940). Germany and United States. Leader in *Gestaltpsychologie.*

377. W. Köhler (1887—   ). G e r m a n y and United States. Leader in *Gestaltpsychologie.*

378. L. Lévy-Bruhl (1860—1940). France. Social psychology.

379. W. McDougall (1871—1938). England and United States. Experimental and social psychology.

380. A. Michotte (1881—   ). Belgian. Experimental Psychology.

381. G. E. Müller (1850—1934). Germany. Pioneer in experimental psychology.

382. I. P. Pavlov (1849—1939). Russia. Conditioned reflex.

383. T. H. Pear (1884—   ). England. Experimental psychology.

384. J. Piaget (1896—   ). Switzerland. Child Psychology.

385. H. Piéron (1881—   ). France. Experimental psychology.

387. E. Rubin (1886—   ). Denmark. Experimental psychology.

388. C. Spearman (1863—1945). England. Experimental psychology.

389. W. Stern (1871—1938). Germany and the United States. Experimental psychology and leader in personalistic psychology.

390. L. M. Terman (1887—   ). United States. Intelligence tests.

391. E. L. Thorndike (1874). United States. Animal and educational psychology.

392. J. B. Watson (1878—   ). United States. Founder of Behaviorism.

393. R. S. Woodworth (1869—   ). United States. Experimental psychology.

394. W. Wundt (1832—1920). Germany. Founder of experimental psychology.

395. R. M. Yerkes (1876—   ). United States. Animal psychology.

354   A. ADLER

355   F. C. BARTLETT

356   W. M. BECHTEREW

357   A. BINET

358   E. G. BORING

359   B. BOURDON

360 C. BURT

361 E. CLAPARÈDE

362 J. DREVER

363 G. TH. FECHNER

364 J. C. FLUGEL

365 S. FREUD

391   E. L. THORNDIKE

392   J. B. WATSON

393   R. S. WOODWORTH

394   W. WUNDT

395   R. M. YERKES

APPENDIX

The author acknowledges his indebtedness to many publishers and psychologists who have generously accorded him permission to include rare photographs and diagrams. Some of the material in this volume is the common property of all psychologists; consequently, acknowledgements are not in order. Unfortunately, the sources of certain of the graphic materials could not be located.

Acknowledgements:

1. and 2. Rauber-Kopsch, *Lehrbuch und Atlas der Anatomie des Menschen,* Vol. 3, 15th Edition. Leipzig, 1939.

3. R. Brun, *Allgemeine Neurosenlehre.* Basle, 1942.

4. R. Höber, *Lehrbuch der Physiologie des Menschen,* 5th Edition. Berlin, 1930.

5. and 6. H. Rohracher, *Die gehirnelektrischen Erscheinungen bei verschiedenen psychischen Vorgängen. Commentationes,* Vol. 1, 1937. Pontifica academia scientiarum

7. W. Nagel, *Handbuch der Physiologie des Menschen.* Braunschweig, 1905.

8. H. Henning, *Der Geruch.* Leipzig, 1916.

9. W. von Buddenbrock, *Die Welt der Sinne.* Berlin, 1932.

10. See No. 7.

11. See No. 7.

12. and 13. W. B. C a n n o n , "Hunger and Thirst" in *A Handbook of General Experimental Psychology.* Worcester, Mass., U. S. A., 1934.

14. and 15. Luciani, *Das Hungern.* Hamburg and Leipzig, 1890.

16. D. Katz, *Animals and Men.* London, 1937.

17. H. Strughold and R. Porz, *Die Dichte der Kaltpunkte auf der Hand des menschlichen Körpers. Zeitschrift für Biologie,* Vol. 91, 1931.

18. See No. 7.

19. G. von Békésy, *Über die Vibrationsempfindung. Akustische Zeitschrift,* 4, 1939.

20. To appear in D. Katz, *Psychologische Übungen.*

21. See No. 20.

22. See No. 7.

23. W. Stern, *Allgemeine Psychologie.* The Hague, 1935.

24. See No. 9.

25. *Zimmermann's Equipment Collection,* Leipzig.

26. See No. 7.

27. H. Kafka, *Handbuch der vergleichenden Physiologie.* Munich, 1922.

28. W. Wundt, *Grundzüge der physiologischen Psychologie.* Vol. 2, Leipzig, 1912.

29. See No. 20.

31. See No. 20.

32. See No. 20.

33. See No. 7.

34. E. Hering, *Grundzüge der Lehre vom Lichtsinn.* Leipzig, 1905.

35. See No. 34.

36. See No. 34.

37. H. v. Helmholtz. *Handbuch der physiologischen Optik.* Hamburg and Leipzig, 1896.

38 - 39. David Katz, *War Greco astigmatisch?* Leipzig, 1914.

40. H. Ebbinghaus, *Grundzüge der Psychologie,* Vol. 2. Leipzig, 1913.

41. See No. 40.

42. See No. 40.

44. See No. 40.

46. See No. 20.

47. See No. 40.

48. See No. 40.

49. David Katz, *Gestaltpsychologie.* B a s l e. 1944.

53. R. Pauli, *Einführung in die experimentelle Psychologie.* Leipzig, 1927.

54. See No. 20.

55. See No. 7.

56. See No. 20.

57. See No. 20.

58. See No. 28.

59. See No. 20.

60. See No. 7.

61. See No. 20.

62. P. J. Young, Reversal of Auditory Localization. Psychological Review.

64. See No. 20.

65. See Nos. 20 and 49.

66. See No. 49.

67. R. S. Woodworth, *Experimental Psychology.* New York, 1938.

68. E. Rubin, *Visuell wahrgenommene Figuren.* Copenhagen, 1921.

69. See No. 20.

70. See No. 49.

73. See No. 49.

74. P. Guilleaume, *Psychologie.* Paris, 1931.

75. Kai von Fieandt; *Über Sehen von Tiefengebilden bei wechselnder Beleuchtung.* Helsinki, 1938.

76. E. Brunswick, *Experimentelle Psychologie in Demonstrationen.* Vienna, 1935.

78. See No. 76.

79 - 80. E. Weigl, *Untersuchungen zur psychischen Umstellbarkeit auf Grund normalpsychologischer und klinischer Befunde.* A report on the 12th Psychological Congress. Jena, 1932.

81. G. Révész, *Die Formenwelt des Tastsinnes.* The Hague, 1938.

82. See No. 16.

83. See No. 16.

84. Fr. Giese, *Die Psychologie der Arbeitshand.* Berlin and Vienna, 1928.

85. G. Révész. *De menschlijke Hand,* 2nd edition. Amsterdam, 1942.

86. See No. 20.

87. See No. 20.

90. Mosso, *Die Ermüdung.* Leipzig, 1922.

93. See No. 20.

94. R. Schulze, *Aus der Werkstatt der experimentellen Psychologie und P ä d a g o g i k.* Leipzig, 1909.

95. See No. 94.

96. See No. 94.

97. See No. 74.

98. See No. 74.

99. See No. 74.

100. See No. 74.

102. J. Obst, *Über graphischen Ausdruck und graphische Sprache.* Rostock, 1938.

103. See No. 67.

104. See No. 67.

105. See No. 67.

106-107. *Zeitschrift für Anatomie und Physiologie.* Berlin, 1908.

108-111. Th. Piderit, *Mimik und Physiognomik.* Detmold, 1886.

112. See No. 74.

139

113-116. Joh. Baptist della Porta, *Physiogno-minia*.

117-118. K ä t h e Olshausen - Schönberger, *Im Spiegel der Tierwelt*. Braun & Schneider, Munich.

119-120. F. K. Walter, *Jahrbuch der Charakterologie*, Vol 4. Berlin, 1927.

121-124. See No. 16.

125-132. See Nos. 121-124.

133-140. Photographs of H. Friesenhahn, a pupil of the author.

141-144. *Encyclopédie française VIII*, "La vie mentale." Paris. 1938.

145-148. E. Kretschmer, *Körperbau und Charakter*, 10th edition. Berlin, 1931.

149. See No. 145.

150-156. Clauss, *Von Seele und Antlitz der Rassen und Völker*, J. F. Lehmanns Verlag, Munich.

157-160. H. Rorschach, *Psychodiagnostik*. Bern, 1937.

161. Lipót Szondi, *Experimentelle Untersuchungen über Neigungen bei Zwillingen*. Budapest, 1940.

162-163. K. Bühler, *Die geistige Entwicklung des Kindes*. Jena, 1924.

164. F. A. Schmidt, *Unser Körper*. Leipzig, 1909.

165. Photograph by med. lic. I n g v a r A l m, Stockholm.

166. Ch. Bühler, *Kindheit und Jugend*. Leipzig, 1931

167. H. Volkelt, *Fortschritte der experimentellen Kinderpsychologie*. Jena, 1926.

168. Harald K. Schjelderup, *Mein Kind ist nervös*. Stockholm, 1938.

169. Arnold Gesell, *I n f a n c y and Human Growth*. New York, 1928.

170. See No. 169.

171-172. H. Lottig, *Hamburger Zwillingsstudien*. Leipzig, 1931.

173. See No. 168.

174. See No. 168.

175. H. Brünning, *Zum 200jährigen Geburtstag eines Wunderkindes*. Monatsschrift für Kinderheilkunde, Vol. 22. 1921.

176. From a drawing by Chodowiecki.

177. James Sully, *Untersuchungen ü b e r d i e Kindheit*. Leipzig 1904. — Cf. also No. 162.

178. F. L. Goodenough, *Measurement of Intelligence by Drawing*. World Book Company, Yonkers, N. Y.

179-182. See No. 177.

183. See No. 177

184. See No. 177.

185. See No. 178.

186. See No. 178.

187. See No. 162.

191. See No. 169.

193. Kik: *Die übernormale Zeichenbegabung bei Kindern*, Zeitschrift für angewandte Psychologie, Vol. 2, 109.

194. See No. 193.

195-196 David Katz: *Ein Beitrag zur Kenntnis der Kinderzeichnungen*, Zeitschrift für Psychologie, Vol. 41. 1906.

197. H. Werner, *Einführung in die Entwicklungspsychologie*. Leipzig, 1926.

198. See No. 167.

199. See No. 167.

200. See No. 167.

201. See No. 162.

203. See No. 162.

204. M. Verworn, *Zur Psychologie der primitiven Kunst*. Jena, 1908.

205. See No. 204.

206. See No. 204.

210. O. Wulff, *Die Kunst des Kindes*. Stuttgart, 1927.

211. See No. 167.

212-215. Rosa Katz, *Das Erziehungssystem der Maria Montessori.* Rostock, 1932.

216-218. Bobertag. *Über Intelligenzprüfungen, Zeitschrift für angewandte Psychologie,* Vol. 5. 1911.

219-220. See No. 20.

221. Van der Torren, *Zeitschrift für angewandte Psychologie,* Vol. 1.

222. Report on the 7th Congress for Experimental Psychology. Jena, 1922.

228. Rosa Katz, *Kinderpsychologische Studien.* Stockholm, 1942.

230-231. See No. 223.

232-234. See No. 223.

235. D. Katz, *Psychologie und mathematischer Unterricht.* Leipzig, 1912.

236. See No. 141.

237. Fr. C. Thiel, *Experimentelle Beiträge zur Lehre vom Vibrationssinn, Zeitschrift für Psychologie.* Vol. 121.

238-239. Richard Paget, *Sign Language as a Form of Speech.* Royal Institution, 1935.

240. See No. 141.

241. See No. 141.

242. See No. 85.

244. From the Home for Blind Deaf-Mutes in Berlin Nowawes.

246-249. See No. 81.

250-253. Ludwig Müntz and Viktor Löwenfeld, *Platische Arbeiten Blinder.* Brünn, 1934.

254-256. C. H. Unthan, *Das Pediskript.* Stuttgart, 1925.

257. *Zeitschrift für orthopädische Chirurgie,* Vol. 50.

258. See No. 257.

259. Photograph by J. Albrecht-Rostock.

260. See No. 20.

261. D. Katz and K. v. Götzen, *Über ein Perkussionphantom. Zeitschrift für Psychologie,* Vol. 108.

262. See No. 49.

263-264. David Katz, *Zur Psychologie des Amputierten und seiner Prothese.* Leipzig, 1921.

265. A. Bethe, *Plastizität und Zentrallehre. Handbuch der normalen und pathologischen Physiologie,* Vol. 15. Berlin, 1931.

266-269. St. Szuman, *Über die im Meskalinrausch bei geschlossenen Augen erscheinenden Visionen. Kwartalnik Psychologiezny,* 1930.

270-273. W. Mayer - Gross, *Psychopathologie und Klinik der Trugwahrnehmungen. Handbuch der Geisteskrankheiten,* Vol. 1. Berlin, 1929.

274. See No. 168.

276. E. Kretschmer, *Medizinische Psychologie,* 6th edition, 1941.

277. Prinzhorn, *Bildnerei der Geisteskranken.* Berlin, 1922.

278. See No. 277.

279. Federn - Meng, *Das psychoanalytische Volksbuch,* 3rd edition. Berlin, 1939.

280. Gustav R. Heyer, *Der Organismus der Seele.* Munich, 1932.

281. See No. 280.

282-283. David Katz, *Animals and Men.* London, 1937.

284. See No. 283.

285. See No. 283.

286. See No. 283.

290-291 A. Sokolowski, *Menschenkunde.* Berlin. Weigandt, *Atlas und Grundriss der Psychiatrie.* Munich 1902.

292. Lévy-Bruhl, *Neue Wege in der Psychiatrie.* Stuttgart, 1925.

293. See No. 292.

294. See No. 292.

295. See No. 292.

297. Ch. Wolff, *Studies in Hand-reading.* London, 1936.

298. See No. 297.

299. D. Katz, *Psychologische Streifzüge.* Stockholm, 1940.

300-301. See No. 299.

302. See No. 299.

303. See No. 299.

304. See No. 299.

305. See No. 299.

306. A. Lehmann, *Aberglaube und Zauberei.* Stuttgart, 1925.

314. W. Moede, *Lehrbuch der Psychotechnik.* Berlin, 1930.

316. See No. 20.

319. Lipmann und Bogen, *Naive Physic,* Leipzig, 1923.

320. W. Blumenfeld, *Eine neue Anstelligkeitsprobe. Zeitschrift für industrielle Psychotechnik.* 1925.

321. *Zeitschrift für Neurologie und Psychiatrie,* Vol. 58, 1920.

325. W. Blumenfeld, *Eignungsprüfung an Lehrlingen der Metallindustrie. Maschinen-Betrieb,* 1923.

326. See No. 314.

327. *Psychotechnical Apparatus.* Zimmermann, Leipzig.

328. L. Edinger, *Über Tierpsychologie.* Leipzig, 1908.

329. Robert M. Yerkes, "The Intelligence of Earthworms." *The Journal of Animal Behavior,* Vol. 2, 1912.

330. W. Fischel, *Tierseelenkunde in Bildern.* Berlin-Lichterfelde, 1932.

331. E. Claparède, *Über Tierpsychologie.* Leipzig, 1908.

332. See No. 16.

333. See No. 331.

334. See No. 16.

335. See No. 16.

336. See No. 16.

337. See No. 16.

338. See No. 16.

339. See No. 16.

341-342. W. Köhler, *Intelligenzprüfungen an Menschenaffen.* Berlin, 1924.

343. E. Claparède, *Tierpsychologie. Handbuch der Naturwissenschaften,* Vol. 9. Jena, 1913.

344. See No. 4.

345. Robert M. Yerkes, *Bahnung und Hemmung der Reaktionen auf taktile Reize durch akustische Reize beim Frosche. Archiv für die gesamte Physiologie,* Vol. 107. 1905.

347. See No. 332.

349. See No. 16.

350. See No. 16.

351-353. See No. 16.